Teach Yourself

D0506562

VISUALLY™

Computers
3rd Edition

Visual™

From

maranGraphics™

&

IDG Books Worldwide, Inc.
An International Data Group Company
Foster City, CA • Indianapolis, IN • Chicago, IL • New York, NY

Teach Yourself VISUALLY™ Computers 3rd Edition

Published by
IDG Books Worldwide, Inc.
An International Data Group Company
909 Third Street
New York, NY 10022

Library of Congress Catalog Card No.: 00-108000

ISBN: 0-7645-3525-0

Printed in the United States of America
10 9 8 7 6 5 4 3 2 1

3K/SX/RS/QQ/MG

Distributed in the United States by IDG Books Worldwide, Inc.

Distributed by CDG Books Canada Inc. for Canada; by Transworld Publishers Limited in the United Kingdom; by IDG Norge Books for Norway; by IDG Sweden Books for Sweden; by IDG Books Australia Publishing Corporation Pty. Ltd. for Australia and New Zealand; by TransQuest Publishers Pte Ltd. for Singapore, Malaysia, Thailand, Indonesia, and Hong Kong; by Gotop Information Inc. for Taiwan; by ICG Muse, Inc. for Japan; by Intersoft for South Africa; by Eyrolles for France; by International Thomson Publishing for Germany, Austria and Switzerland; by Distribuidora Cuspide for Argentina; by LR International for Brazil; by Galileo Libros for Chile; by Ediciones ZETA S.C.R. Ltda. for Peru; by WS Computer Publishing Corporation, Inc. for the Philippines; by Contemporanea de Ediciones for Venezuela; by Express Computer Distributors for the Caribbean and West Indies; by Micronesia Media Distributor, Inc. for Micronesia; by Chips Computadoras S.A. de C.V. for Mexico; by Editorial Norma de Panama S.A. for Panama; by American Bookshops for Finland.
For corporate orders, please call maranGraphics at 800-469-6616.
For general information on IDG Books Worldwide's books in the U.S., please call our Consumer Customer Service department at 800-762-2974.
For reseller information, including discounts and premium sales, please call our Reseller Customer Service department at 800-434-3422.
For information on where to purchase IDG Books Worldwide's books outside the U.S., please contact our International Sales department at 317-572-3993 or fax 317-572-4002.
For consumer information on foreign language translations, please contact our Customer Service department at 800-434-3422, fax 800-550-2747, or e-mail rights@idgbooks.com.
For information on licensing foreign or domestic rights, please phone 650-653-7000 of fax 650-653-7500.
For sales inquiries and special prices for bulk quantities, please contact our Sales department at 650-655-3200.
For information on using IDG Books Worldwide's books in the classroom or for ordering examination copies, please contact our Educational Sales department at 800-434-2086 or fax 317-572-4005.
For press review copies, author interviews, or other publicity information, please contact our Public Relations department at 650-653-7000 or fax 650-653-7500.
For authorization to photocopy items for corporate, personal, or educational use, please contact maranGraphics at 800-469-6616.

Trademark Acknowledgments

Permissions

ABOUT IDG BOOKS WORLDWIDE

Welcome to the world of IDG Books Worldwide.

IDG Books Worldwide, Inc., is a subsidiary of International Data Group, the world's largest publisher of computer-related information and the leading global provider of information services on information technology. IDG was founded more than 30 years ago by Patrick J. McGovern and now employs more than 9,000 people worldwide. IDG publishes more than 290 computer publications in over 75 countries. More than 90 million people read one or more IDG publications each month.

Launched in 1990, IDG Books Worldwide is today the #1 publisher of best-selling computer books in the United States. We are proud to have received eight awards from the Computer Press Association in recognition of editorial excellence and three from Computer Currents' First Annual Readers' Choice Awards. Our best-selling ...For Dummies® series has more than 50 million copies in print with translations in 31 languages. IDG Books Worldwide, through a joint venture with IDG's Hi-Tech Beijing, became the first U.S. publisher to publish a computer book in the People's Republic of China. In record time, IDG Books Worldwide has become the first choice for millions of readers around the world who want to learn how to better manage their businesses.

Our mission is simple: Every one of our books is designed to bring extra value and skill-building instructions to the reader. Our books are written by experts who understand and care about our readers. The knowledge base of our editorial staff comes from years of experience in publishing, education, and journalism — experience we use to produce books to carry us into the new millennium. In short, we care about books, so we attract the best people. We devote special attention to details such as audience, interior design, use of icons, and illustrations. And because we use an efficient process of authoring, editing, and desktop publishing our books electronically, we can spend more time ensuring superior content and less time on the technicalities of making books.

You can count on our commitment to deliver high-quality books at competitive prices on topics you want to read about. At IDG Books Worldwide, we continue in the IDG tradition of delivering quality for more than 30 years. You'll find no better book on a subject than one from IDG Books Worldwide.

John Kilcullen
Chairman and CEO
IDG Books Worldwide, Inc.

Eighth Annual
Computer Press
Awards ≥1992

Ninth Annual
Computer Press
Awards ≥1993

Tenth Annual
Computer Press
Awards ≥ 1994

Eleventh Annual
Computer Press
Awards ≥1995

IDG is the world's leading IT media, research and exposition company. Founded in 1964, IDG had 1997 revenues of $2.05 billion and has more than 9,000 employees worldwide. IDG offers the widest range of media options that reach IT buyers in 75 countries representing 95% of worldwide IT spending. IDG's diverse product and services portfolio spans six key areas including print publishing, online publishing, expositions and conferences, market research, education and training, and global marketing services. More than 90 million people read one or more of IDG's 290 magazines and newspapers, including IDG's leading global brands — Computerworld, PC World, Network World, Macworld and the Channel World family of publications. IDG Books Worldwide is one of the fastest-growing computer book publishers in the world, with more than 700 titles in 36 languages. The "...For Dummies®" series alone has more than 50 million copies in print. IDG offers online users the largest network of technology-specific Web sites around the world through IDG.net (http://www.idg.net), which comprises more than 225 targeted Web sites in 55 countries worldwide. International Data Corporation (IDC) is the world's largest provider of information technology data, analysis and consulting, with research centers in over 41 countries and more than 400 research analysts worldwide. IDG World Expo is a leading producer of more than 168 globally branded conferences and expositions in 35 countries including E3 (Electronic Entertainment Expo), Macworld Expo, ComNet, Windows World Expo, ICE (Internet Commerce Expo), Agenda, DEMO, and Spotlight. IDG's training subsidiary, ExecuTrain, is the world's largest computer training company, with more than 230 locations worldwide and 785 training courses. IDG Marketing Services helps industry-leading IT companies build international brand recognition by developing global integrated marketing programs via IDG's print, online and exposition products worldwide. Further information about the company can be found at www.idg.com. 1/26/00

maranGraphics is a family-run business
located near Toronto, Canada.

At **maranGraphics**, we believe in producing great computer books–one book at a time.

Each maranGraphics book uses the award-winning communication process that we have been developing over the last 25 years. Using this process, we organize screen shots, text and illustrations in a way that makes it easy for you to learn new concepts and tasks.

We spend hours deciding the best way to perform each task, so you don't have to! Our clear, easy-to-follow screen shots and instructions walk you through each task from beginning to end.

Our detailed illustrations go hand-in-hand with the text to help reinforce the information. Each illustration is a labor of love–some take up to a week to draw!

We want to thank you for purchasing what we feel are the best computer books money can buy. We hope you enjoy using this book as much as we enjoyed creating it!

Sincerely,

The Maran Family

Please visit us on the Web at:
www.maran.com

CREDITS

Authors:
Ruth Maran
Paul Whitehead

Copy Editors:
Cathy Benn
Roxanne Van Damme

Project Manager:
Judy Maran

Editors:
Teri Lynn Pinsent
James Menzies
Norm Schumacher

**Layout Designer &
Illustrator:**
Treena Lees

Illustrators:
Russ Marini
Sean Johannesen
Dave Thornhill
Natalie Tweedie

Indexer:
Teri Lynn Pinsent

Permissions Coordinator:
Jennifer Amaral

**Senior Vice President and
Publisher, IDG Books
Technology Publishing
Group:**
Richard Swadley

**Publishing Director,
IDG Books Technology
Publishing Group:**
Barry Pruett

**Editorial Support,
IDG Books Technology
Publishing Group:**
Martine Edwards
Lindsay Sandman
Sandy Rodrigues

**Post Production &
Technical Consultant:**
Robert Maran

ACKNOWLEDGMENTS

Thanks to the dedicated staff of maranGraphics, including
Jennifer Amaral, Roderick Anatalio, Cathy Benn, Sean Johannesen,
Kelleigh Johnson, Wanda Lawrie, Luis Lee, Treena Lees, Jill Maran,
Judy Maran, Robert Maran, Ruth Maran, Russ Marini, James Menzies,
Suzana G. Miokovic, Stacey Morrison, Teri Lynn Pinsent,
Steven Schaerer, Norm Schumacher, Raquel Scott, Dave Thornhill,
Natalie Tweedie, Roxanne Van Damme and Paul Whitehead.

Finally, to Richard Maran who originated the easy-to-use
graphic format of this guide. Thank you for your
inspiration and guidance.

TABLE OF CONTENTS

Chapter 1

INTRODUCTION TO COMPUTERS

Chapter 2

INPUT AND OUTPUT DEVICES

Chapter 3

PROCESSING

Chapter 4

STORAGE DEVICES

Chapter 5

SOFTWARE

TABLE OF CONTENTS

Chapter 6

OPERATING SYSTEMS

Chapter 7

PORTABLE COMPUTERS

Chapter 8

MACINTOSH COMPUTERS

Chapter 9

NETWORKS

Chapter 10

THE INTERNET

TABLE OF CONTENTS

Chapter 11

THE WORLD WIDE WEB

Chapter 12

ELECTRONIC MAIL AND MAILING LISTS

Chapter 13

NEWSGROUPS AND CHAT

Chapter 14

MULTIMEDIA DEVICES

Chapter 15

WIRELESS DEVICES

Chapter 16

VISUAL GLOSSARY

CHAPTER 1

Introduction to Computers

Do you want to learn more about your computer? This chapter will help you get started.

HARDWARE AND SOFTWARE

HARDWARE

Hardware and software are the two basic parts of a computer system.

Hardware is any part of a computer system you can see or touch.

Peripheral

A peripheral is any piece of hardware attached to a computer, such as a printer.

SOFTWARE

Software is a set of electronic instructions that tell a computer what to do. You cannot see or touch software, but you can see and touch the packaging the software comes in.

Application Software

Application software allows you to accomplish specific tasks. Popular application software includes Microsoft Word and Intuit Quicken.

Operating System Software

Operating system software controls the overall activity of a computer. Most new computers come with the Windows Me operating system software.

GETTING HELP

There are many ways to get help when using new hardware and software.

DOCUMENTATION

Hardware and software should include documentation that tells you how to set up and use the product. Many software packages also come with a built-in help feature. You can also check local book stores for manuals with detailed, step-by-step instructions.

CONSULT THE EXPERTS

If you have questions about setting up or using new hardware or software, try calling the store where you purchased the product. You can also visit the manufacturer's Web site on the Internet for more information about the product.

CLASSES

Colleges and computer stores often offer computer courses. Many communities also have computer clubs where you can ask questions and exchange ideas.

HOW COMPUTERS WORK

A computer collects, processes, stores and outputs information.

INPUT

An input device lets you communicate with a computer. You can use input devices to enter information and issue commands. A keyboard, mouse and joystick are input devices.

PROCESS

The Central Processing Unit (CPU) is the main chip in a computer. The CPU processes instructions, performs calculations and manages the flow of information through a computer system. The CPU communicates with input, output and storage devices to perform tasks.

STORE

A storage device reads and records information on storage media. The computer uses information stored on the storage media to perform tasks. Popular examples of storage devices include a hard drive, floppy drive, CD-R drive, tape drive and DVD-ROM drive.

OUTPUT

An output device lets a computer communicate with you. These devices display information on a screen, create printed copies or generate sound. A monitor, printer and speakers are output devices.

Bytes are used to measure
the amount of information
a device can store.

Byte

One byte is one character. A
character can be a number,
letter or symbol. One byte
consists of eight bits (binary
digits). A bit is the smallest
unit of information a computer
can process.

Kilobyte (KB)

One kilobyte is
1,024 characters.
This is approximately
equal to one page of
double-spaced text.

Megabyte (MB)

One megabyte is
1,048,576 characters.
This is approximately
equal to one book.

Gigabyte (GB)

One gigabyte is 1,073,741,824
characters. This is approximately
equal to a shelf of books in a
library.

Terabyte (TB)

One terabyte is 1,099,511,627,776
characters. This is approximately
equal to an entire library of books.

TYPES OF COMPUTER SYSTEMS

There are several types of computer systems.

PC

A PC (Personal Computer) is a computer designed to meet the needs of an individual and usually refers to IBM-compatible computers. PCs are found in many businesses and are popular for home use.

MACINTOSH

Macintosh computers are found in many homes and are very popular in the graphics, publishing and multimedia industries. The Macintosh was the first home computer that offered a graphical display.

MAINFRAME

A mainframe is a computer that can process and store large amounts of information and support many users at the same time. A terminal, consisting of a keyboard and monitor, is used to input and output information on a mainframe.

SET-TOP BOX

A set-top box is a computer device that connects to your television. Set-top boxes allow you to use your telephone line or cable connection to browse the Internet and exchange electronic mail on your television.

A typical computer system consists of several parts.

Computer Case

A computer case contains the major components of a computer system.

Monitor

A monitor is a device that displays text and images generated by the computer.

Printer

A printer is a device that produces a paper copy of documents you create on the computer.

Speakers

Speakers are devices that play sound generated by the computer.

Modem

A modem is a device that lets computers communicate through telephone lines. A modem can be found inside or outside the computer case.

Keyboard

A keyboard is a device that lets you type information and instructions into a computer.

Mouse

A mouse is a handheld device that lets you select and move items on the screen.

INSIDE A COMPUTER

All computers
contain the same
basic components.

Power Supply

A power supply changes
normal household
electricity into electricity
that a computer can use.

Hard Drive

A hard drive is the primary
device that a computer
uses to store information.

Port

A port is a connector
where you plug in an
external device such
as a printer.

Expansion Card

An expansion card lets you add
new features to a computer. For
example, an expansion card
can give a computer the ability
to record and play sound.

Expansion Slot

An expansion slot is a
socket on the system
board. An expansion
card plugs into an
expansion slot.

System Board

A system board is the main
circuit board of a computer.
All electrical components
plug into the system board.

CD-ROM or DVD-ROM Drive

A CD-ROM drive reads information stored on Compact Discs (CDs). A DVD-ROM drive reads information stored on CDs and Digital Versatile Discs (DVDs).

Floppy Drive

A floppy drive stores and retrieves information on floppy disks.

Drive Bay

A drive bay is a space inside the computer case where a hard drive, floppy drive, CD-ROM drive or DVD-ROM drive sits.

Central Processing Unit (CPU)

A CPU is the main chip in a computer. The CPU processes instructions, performs calculations and manages the flow of information through a computer.

Random Access Memory (RAM)

RAM temporarily stores information inside a computer. This information is lost when you turn off the computer.

COMPUTER CASE

A computer case contains the major components of a computer system.

Desktop Case

A desktop case usually sits on a desk, under a monitor.

Tower Case

A tower case usually sits on the floor. This provides more desk space, but can be less convenient for inserting and removing items such as floppy disks and CD-ROM discs. Tower cases come in different sizes.

NOTEBOOK

A notebook is a small, lightweight computer that you can easily transport. A notebook computer has a built-in keyboard and screen.

ALL-IN-ONE CASE

An all-in-one case contains a monitor, hard drive, CD-ROM drive and speakers in a single unit.

POWER SUPPLY

A power supply changes the alternating current (AC) that comes from an outlet to the direct current (DC) that a computer can use.

The capacity of a power supply is measured in watts. An average computer uses up to 250 watts, whereas an average light bulb uses 60 watts.

A fan inside the power supply prevents the parts inside a computer from overheating.

PROTECT YOUR EQUIPMENT

Changes in electrical power can damage equipment and information.

Surge Protector

A surge protector, or surge suppressor, guards a computer against surges. A surge is a fluctuation in power. These fluctuations happen most often during storms.

UPS

An Uninterruptible Power Supply (UPS) protects a computer from a loss of power. A UPS contains a battery that stores electrical power. If the power fails, the battery can run the computer for a short time so you can save your information.

PORT

A port is a connector where you plug in an external device such as a printer. This allows instructions and data to flow between the computer and the device.

Keyboard Port

A keyboard port connects a keyboard. A keyboard port can come in two sizes.

Mouse Port

A mouse port connects a mouse.

Parallel Port

A parallel port has 25 holes. This type of port is known as a female connector. A parallel port usually connects a printer or an external storage device.

A computer internally labels each parallel port with the letters LPT. The first parallel port is named LPT1, the second parallel port is named LPT2, and so on.

There are two enhanced types of parallel ports–Enhanced Parallel Port (EPP) and Extended Capabilities Port (ECP). These types of parallel ports increase the speed at which information flows between the computer and a device.

Monitor Port

A monitor port connects a monitor.

USB Port

Universal Serial Bus (USB) is a type of port that allows you to connect up to 127 devices using only one port. For example, you can use a USB port to connect a printer, modem, joystick and scanner to your computer. Most new computers come with two USB ports.

Serial Port

A serial port has either 9 or 25 pins. This type of port is known as a male connector. A serial port can connect a mouse or external modem.

A computer internally labels each serial port with the letters COM. The first serial port is named COM1, the second serial port is named COM2, and so on.

Network Port

A network port is found on a network interface card and allows you to connect the computer to a network.

Game Port

A game port connects a joystick or other game controller.

EXPANSION CARD

An expansion card is a circuit board that lets you add new features to a computer.

An expansion card is also called an expansion board.

EXPANSION SLOT

An expansion slot is a socket where you plug in an expansion card.

The number of expansion slots your computer has affects the number of features you can add to the computer. Before you buy a computer, make sure it has enough empty expansion slots for your future needs.

CONNECT DEVICES

Most expansion cards contain ports where you can plug in devices. For example, you can plug speakers into a sound card to hear sound generated by the computer. The ports on an expansion card are usually accessible from the back of a computer.

COMMON EXPANSION CARD TYPES

A computer usually comes with one or more expansion cards.

Video

A video card generates the images displayed on the monitor.

Modem

A modem card lets computers exchange information through telephone lines.

Sound

A sound card lets a computer play and record sound.

Network Interface

A network interface card lets connected computers share information and equipment.

PURCHASE A NEW COMPUTER

There are many factors to consider when purchasing a new computer.

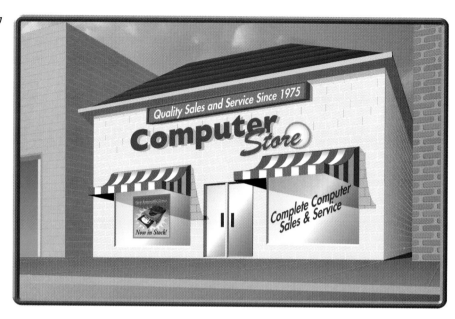

You should purchase a computer from a business with a good reputation that has been in operation for a number of years.

CONSIDERATIONS

Cost

The cost of a computer depends on your needs. You can purchase a basic home computer for under $800. If you want a computer better able to handle complex tasks, such as running multimedia applications, you will need to spend more money.

In many cases, a monitor is not included in the price of a computer.

Brand-name and Clone Computers

When purchasing a new computer, you can choose either a brand-name or a clone computer. Brand-name computers are made by large manufacturers, such as IBM or Apple. Clone computers are made by independent manufacturers. Clone computers function exactly like brand-name computers, but are usually less expensive.

After-sale Service

You should make sure the computer you purchase comes with after-sale service. After-sale service should include a one or two-year warranty on computer parts and labor, as well as telephone technical support.

UPGRADE A COMPUTER

You can upgrade a computer to enhance the computer's performance. For many upgrades, you will need the assistance of an experienced computer repairperson.

Upgrading usually refers to replacing an old or obsolete component with a newer component to improve the efficiency of the computer. Upgrading can also include adding a new component, such as a DVD-ROM drive, to increase the capabilities of the computer.

CONSIDERATIONS

Cost

You should always determine the cost of an upgrade before performing the upgrade. If you are planning a major upgrade, such as replacing the system board or CPU, it may be less expensive to purchase a new computer.

Effective Upgrades

Increasing the amount of memory in a computer is one of the most effective upgrades you can perform. Doubling the existing memory in a computer can significantly increase the performance of the computer.

ERGONOMICS

Ergonomics is the science of designing equipment for a safe and comfortable working environment.

PREVENT BACK AND NECK STRAIN

You can avoid back and neck strain by ensuring that your chair provides proper support and by placing the monitor where you can comfortably view the screen.

Monitor Placement

The top edge of the monitor should be at eye level or slightly lower. You can use a monitor stand or telephone book to raise the monitor to the appropriate level on your desk.

Posture

When seated, make sure your feet are flat on the floor and you do not lean forward or slouch in your chair. You should shift positions often and stand up to stretch your arms and legs at least once an hour.

Chair

Look for a fully adjustable chair that provides support for your lower back. Contoured chair seats help blood circulate more freely by relieving pressure on the legs.

PREVENT WRIST STRAIN

To prevent wrist strain when typing, keep your elbows level with the keyboard and your wrists straight and higher than your fingers. When using a mouse, move the mouse with your entire arm instead of just your wrist.

Carpal Tunnel Syndrome (CTS)

Carpal tunnel syndrome is a Repetitive Stress Injury (RSI) whose symptoms include numbness, tingling and pain in the fingers. This condition affects some people who type without proper wrist support or who type for long periods of time without breaks.

Wrist Rest

You can use a wrist rest with your keyboard to elevate your wrists and ensure they remain straight. Some mouse pads also come with built-in wrist rests.

PREVENT EYESTRAIN

Monitor Position

Position your monitor at a comfortable viewing distance and in a way that minimizes reflections and glare. To further reduce glare, you may want to use a glare filter that fits over the front of the monitor.

Frequent Breaks

You should frequently relax your eyes by looking away from your monitor and focusing on items that are far away.

CHAPTER 2

Input and Output Devices

What is a high-speed Internet connection and why would you want one? What type of printer is best for you? This chapter will answer these questions and more.

MOUSE

A mouse is a handheld pointing device that lets you select and move items on your screen.

A mouse can come in various shapes, colors and sizes.

USE THE MOUSE

Resting your hand on the mouse, use your thumb and two rightmost fingers to move the mouse on the desk. Use your two remaining fingers to press the mouse buttons.

When you move the mouse on your desk, the pointer on the screen moves in the same direction. The pointer assumes different shapes (example: ⌖ or ⌶) depending on its location on the screen and the task you are performing.

MOUSE PAD

A mouse pad provides a smooth surface for moving a mouse and reduces the amount of dirt that enters the mouse. You can buy mouse pads displaying interesting designs or pictures at most computer stores. Some mouse pads have built-in wrist support for increased comfort.

MOUSE ACTIONS

Click

A click often selects an item on the screen. To click, press and release the left mouse button.

Double-click

A double-click often opens a document or starts a program. To double-click, quickly press and release the left mouse button twice.

Right-click

A right-click often displays a list of commands on the screen. To right-click, press and release the right mouse button.

Drag and Drop

Dragging and dropping makes it easy to move an item on the screen. Position the pointer over an item on the screen and then press and hold down the left mouse button. Still holding down the button, move the pointer to where you want to place the item and then release the button.

LEFT-HANDED USERS

If you are left-handed, you can switch the functions of the left and right mouse buttons to make the mouse easier to use. For example, to click an item, you would press the right button instead of the left.

CLEAN THE MOUSE

If there is a ball inside your mouse, you should occasionally remove and clean the ball. Make sure you also remove dust and dirt from the inside to help ensure smooth motion of the mouse.

MOUSE

There are several advanced mouse types available that offer useful features.

Wheeled Mouse

A wheeled mouse has a wheel between the left and right mouse buttons. You can often use this wheel to scroll through information or zoom in and out. The Microsoft IntelliMouse is a popular example of a wheeled mouse.

Wireless Mouse

A wireless, or cordless, mouse runs on a battery and reduces the clutter on your desk by eliminating the mouse cord. When you move the mouse on your desk, the mouse sends signals to your computer, the same way a remote control sends signals to a television.

Programmable Mouse

You can purchase a mouse that has buttons you can program to perform specific tasks, such as double-clicking an item. A three-button mouse is an example of a programmable mouse.

Optical Sensor Mouse

An optical sensor mouse detects mouse movement using an optical sensor rather than a ball inside the mouse. This type of mouse does not contain any moving parts that can wear out or stick. A mouse pad is not required when using an optical sensor mouse.

OTHER POINTING DEVICES

Touchpad

A touchpad is a surface that is sensitive to pressure and motion. When you move your fingertip across the pad, the pointer on the screen moves in the same direction.

Trackball

A trackball is an upside-down mouse that remains stationary on your desk. You roll the ball with your fingers or palm to move the pointer on the screen. A trackball is a great alternative to a mouse when you have limited desk space.

Pointing Stick

A pointing stick resembles the eraser on the end of a pencil. The mouse pointer moves in the direction you push the pointing stick. Pointing sticks also have buttons, similar to mouse buttons, you can press to perform an action such as a click.

KEYBOARD

The keys on a keyboard let you enter information and instructions into a computer.

Most keyboards have 101 keys. Your keyboard may look different than the keyboard shown here.

Escape Key

You can press **Esc** to quit a task you are performing.

Programmable Buttons

Many new keyboards have buttons you can program to perform tasks such as connecting to the Internet, adjusting multimedia settings and more.

Function Keys

These keys let you quickly perform specific tasks. For example, in many programs you can press **F1** to display help information.

Caps Lock and Shift Keys

These keys let you enter text in uppercase (ABC) and lowercase (abc) letters.

Press **Caps Lock** to change the case of all letters you type. Press the key again to return to the original case.

Press **Shift** in combination with another key to type an uppercase letter.

Ctrl and Alt Keys

You can use the **Ctrl** or **Alt** key in combination with another key to perform a specific task. For example, in some programs you can press **Ctrl** and **S** to save a document.

Windows Key

You can press the **Windows** key to quickly display the Start menu when using a Windows operating system, such as Windows Me or Windows 2000.

Spacebar

You can press the **Spacebar** to insert a blank space.

Backspace Key

You can press **Backspace** to remove the character to the left of the cursor.

Delete Key

You can press **Delete** to remove the character to the right of the cursor.

Status Lights

These lights indicate whether the **Num Lock** and **Caps Lock** features are on or off.

Numeric Keypad

When the **Num Lock** light is on, you can use the number keys (0 through 9) to enter numbers. When the **Num Lock** light is off, you can use these keys to move the cursor around the screen. To turn the light on or off, press **Num Lock**.

Application Key

You can press the **Application** key to quickly display the shortcut menu for an item on your screen.

Enter Key

You can press **Enter** to tell the computer to carry out a task. In a word processing program, press this key to start a new paragraph.

Arrow Keys

These keys let you move the cursor around the screen.

KEYBOARD

TYPES OF KEYBOARDS

Wireless

Wireless, or cordless, keyboards do not use a cable to connect to a computer. A wireless keyboard runs on a battery and sends signals to your computer, the same way a remote control sends signals to a television.

Built-In Enhancements

Many new keyboards include built-in enhancements such as touchpads, microphones, speakers, volume controls and buttons that allow you to quickly access the Internet.

Ergonomic

Ergonomically designed keyboards position your hands naturally and support your wrists so you can work more comfortably.

CLEAN A KEYBOARD

Over time, dust and dirt can accumulate on a keyboard, causing the keys to stick or not respond when pressed. To remove dust and dirt, you can run a vacuum cleaner over the keys.

The plastic outer surface of the keyboard can be cleaned with a damp cloth. You should not attempt to open your keyboard to clean the inside, as this can damage the keyboard.

KEYBOARD TIPS

Typing Programs

There are programs available to help you improve your typing skills. You can buy these programs at most computer stores.

Position Your Hands

Most keyboards have small bumps on the F and J keys. These bumps help you position your fingers without looking at the keyboard.

Special Characters

Many programs let you enter special characters or symbols that do not appear on the keyboard. For example, you can type **(C)** in some programs to create the © symbol.

Keyboard Shortcuts

Most programs let you select commands by using keyboard shortcuts. These shortcuts are often shown on the menus. For example, to select the **Save** command in some programs, you can press the **Ctrl** and **S** keys.

A plus sign (+) between two key names tells you to press and hold down the first key before pressing the second key.

A printer produces a paper copy of the information displayed on the screen.

You can buy a printer that produces black-and-white or color images.

You can use a printer to produce letters, invoices, newsletters, transparencies, labels, packing slips and much more.

CHOOSE A PRINTER

There are several factors to consider when buying a printer.

■ Make sure the printer will work with your computer and software.

■ Check the size and type of paper the printer accepts. Some printers can print on large sheets of paper.

■ Check the cost of materials such as ink and paper.

■ Check the amount of paper the printer tray can hold.

■ If you want to print on envelopes, transparencies or labels, make sure the printer will accept these items.

DOT-MATRIX PRINTER

A dot-matrix printer produces low-quality images. Inside a dot-matrix printer, a print head containing small, blunt pins strikes an inked ribbon. This is useful for printing on multipart forms that need an impact to print through multiple copies.

LED PRINTER

A Light Emitting Diode (LED) printer produces images on a page by using several small lights. LED printers can print pages that are comparable in quality to laser printers, but LED printers are less expensive. For information on laser printers, see page 36.

COLOR PHOTO PRINTER

A color photo printer is designed to produce photographic-quality images. This type of printer usually requires a special type of paper and may only accept paper in standard photographic sizes, such as 4 x 6.

MULTIFUNCTION PRINTER

A multifunction printer can perform more than one task. This type of printer is often able to work as a fax machine, scanner and photocopier, as well as a printer. Color multifunction printers are also available.

PRINTER

INK-JET PRINTER

An ink-jet printer produces high-quality documents at a relatively low price. This type of printer is ideal for routine business and personal documents.

An ink-jet printer has a print head that sprays ink through small nozzles onto a page.

Speed

The speed of a printer is measured in pages per minute (ppm) and determines how quickly a printer can produce pages. A higher speed results in faster output.

Most ink-jet printers can produce images at a speed of 2 to 10 pages per minute (ppm).

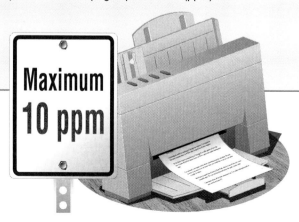

Resolution

The resolution of a printer determines the quality of images it can produce. A higher resolution results in sharper, more detailed images. Printer resolution is measured in dots per inch (dpi). Ink-jet printers can have a resolution ranging from 360 to 2400 dots per inch (dpi).

Resolution is sometimes expressed with two numbers (example: 600 x 600 dpi). These numbers describe the number of dots a printer can produce across and down one square inch.

Ink

Ink-jet printers use ink stored in cartridges. When the ink runs out, you replace the cartridge. You may also be able to refill a cartridge with ink. You should always use the printer manufacturer's recommended cartridges or ink for best results.

Many ink cartridges have an expiry date on them. Before you buy a new cartridge, you should make sure it has not expired.

Paper

Ink-jet printers accept 8 1/2 by 11-inch paper. Some ink-jet printers also accept larger paper, envelopes, labels and transparencies. Make sure you buy items designed specifically for ink-jet printers.

Ink-jet printers can use standard paper, but printing quality improves when you use more expensive, coated paper. Some ink-jet printers can also use special glossy paper to produce photographic quality images.

Color

Color ink-jet printers are very popular because they are less expensive than other types of color printers and still produce high-quality color images. A color ink-jet printer sprays cyan, magenta, yellow and black ink to create different colors on a page.

PRINTER

LASER PRINTER

A laser printer is a high-speed printer that is ideal for business and personal documents and for professional graphics work.

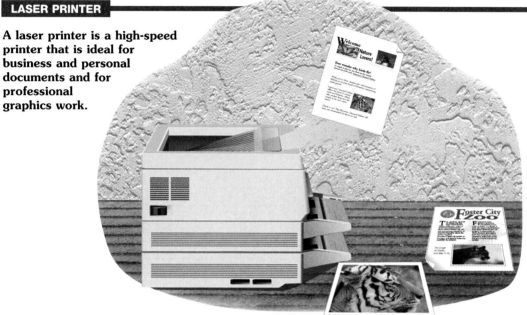

A laser printer works like a photocopier to produce high-quality images on a page.

Speed

Most laser printers produce images at a speed of 4 to 16 pages per minute (ppm).

All laser printers have a Central Processing Unit (CPU) that processes instructions and manages the flow of information in the printer. The CPU speed is a major factor in determining how fast a laser printer operates. The faster the CPU speed, the faster the printer will produce images.

Resolution

The resolution, or quality, of the images produced by a laser printer ranges from 600 to 2400 dots per inch (dpi).

Memory

Laser printers store pages in built-in memory before printing. A typical laser printer comes with 2 to 8 MB of memory.

Memory is important for laser printers that produce images at high resolutions, such as 2400 dpi. Memory is also important for laser printers that print on larger paper sizes and process complex print jobs.

Toner

Like photocopiers, laser printers use a fine powdered ink, called toner, which comes in a cartridge. When the toner runs out, you buy a new cartridge. Check the documentation that came with the printer to determine which type of cartridge the printer can use.

Paper

All laser printers can print on 8 1/2 by 11-inch paper, envelopes, labels and transparencies. For best results, check the printer's documentation to find the size, composition and weight of the paper the printer can use.

Color

You can buy laser printers that produce color images. A color laser printer is more expensive than a color ink jet printer, but it produces superior output.

MONITOR AND VIDEO CARD

The monitor and video card work together to display text and images on the screen.

Screen

The screen is the display area of a monitor.

Monitor

A monitor displays text and images generated by the video card.

A cable connects the monitor to the video card in the computer.

Video Card

A video card is a circuit board that plugs into an expansion slot inside the computer. A video card translates instructions from the computer into a form the monitor can understand.

A video card is also called a video adapter, graphics adapter or graphics card.

Some computers do not need a video card, since they have video capabilities built into the system board.

MONITOR CONSIDERATIONS

Size

The size of a monitor is measured diagonally across the screen. Common monitor sizes are 14, 15, 17 and 21 inches. Larger monitors are more expensive and are ideal for desktop publishing and working with graphics or large spreadsheets.

Manufacturers usually advertise the diagonal measurement of the picture tube inside the monitor, which is greater than the actual viewing area. Make sure you ask for the size of the viewing area.

Flat-panel

A flat-panel monitor uses Liquid Crystal Display (LCD), which is the same type of display found in most digital wristwatches. In the past, flat-panel screens were only used on portable computers, but now full-size flat-panel monitors are available for desktop computers.

Flat-panel monitors are more expensive than regular monitors, but are lighter, take up less desk space and use less electricity.

Dot Pitch

The dot pitch is the distance between pixels on a screen. A pixel is the smallest element on a screen. The dot pitch determines the sharpness of images on the screen and is measured in millimeters (mm).

The smaller the dot pitch, the crisper the images. Select a monitor with a dot pitch of 0.28 mm or less.

MONITOR AND VIDEO CARD

Refresh Rate

The refresh rate determines the speed that a monitor redraws, or updates, images. The higher the refresh rate, the less flicker on the screen. This helps reduce eyestrain.

The refresh rate is measured in hertz (Hz) and tells you the number of times per second the monitor redraws the entire screen. A monitor with a refresh rate of 72 Hz or more is recommended.

Controls

Monitors have controls to adjust the brightness, contrast and other features of the images displayed on the screen. You can find controls on the screen or on the monitor.

Tilt-and-swivel Base

A tilt-and-swivel base lets you adjust the angle of the screen. This lets you reduce the glare from overhead lighting and view the screen more comfortably.

Electromagnetic Radiation

Any device that uses electricity produces Electromagnetic Radiation (EMR). You can minimize the risk of EMR by buying a monitor that meets MPR II guidelines. The MPR II guidelines define acceptable levels of EMR.

You can further minimize the risk by sitting a safe distance away from your monitor and turning off the monitor when it is not in use.

The manual that came with your monitor may provide information about the EMR produced by the monitor and offer suggestions for protecting yourself from its potentially harmful effects.

Energy Star

The Environmental Protection Agency (EPA) developed an energy-saving guideline called ENERGY STAR to reduce wasted energy and the pollution it causes.

When you do not use an ENERGY STAR computer for a period of time, the monitor and computer enter an energy-saving sleep mode. You awaken the computer by moving the mouse or pressing a key on the keyboard.

MONITOR AND VIDEO CARD

Screen Saver

A screen saver is a moving picture or pattern that appears on the screen when you do not use a computer for a period of time.

Screen savers were originally designed to prevent screen burn, which occurs when an image appears in a fixed position for a period of time. Today's monitors are designed to prevent screen burn, but people still use screen savers for entertainment.

The Windows operating system provides several screen savers. You can also purchase screen savers at most computer stores.

Using a process called Webcasting, you can also use screen savers that display customized, up-to-the-minute information. This information is transferred to your computer over the Internet.

Glare Filter

A glare filter fits over the front of a monitor to reduce the amount of light reflected off the computer screen. This helps reduce eyestrain.

A glare filter may be able to block the radiation coming from the front of the monitor. Some glare filters make the screen difficult to read when viewed from an angle, which can help you keep your work private.

VIDEO CARD CONSIDERATIONS

Video Card Memory

A video card has memory chips. These chips temporarily store information before sending it to the monitor.

Most computers require at least 2 MB of video card memory.

AGP

An Accelerated Graphics Port (AGP) video card uses an AGP bus to communicate directly with your computer's main memory. This allows you to quickly display complex images on your monitor.

AGP is specially designed to meet the high demands of displaying 3D images.

3D Graphics Accelerator Card

A 3D graphics accelerator card has a specialized chip, called a Graphics Processing Unit (GPU), that is optimized to produce 3D graphics. A GPU allows a video card to display information on the screen without using your computer's processor.

This type of video card is required for playing some graphic intensive games that display 3D images.

MONITOR AND VIDEO CARD

Refresh Rate

Your video card must be able to use the same refresh rate as your monitor. Most monitors can detect which refresh rate the video card is using and then automatically switch to the appropriate setting.

Color Depth

The video card you use determines the number of colors a monitor can display. More colors result in more realistic images.

16 Colors (4-bit color)

Choppy-looking images.

256 Colors (8-bit color)

Suitable for most home, business and game applications.

65,536 Colors (16-bit color)

Useful for video and desktop publishing applications. Unless you are a trained professional, it is difficult to distinguish between 16-bit and 24-bit color.

16,777,216 Colors (24-bit color)

Useful for photographic work. This setting is also called true color because it displays more colors than the human eye can distinguish.

16,777,216 Colors (32-bit color)

Useful for graphic intensive games. This setting works more efficiently and faster than 24-bit color.

RESOLUTION

Resolution determines the amount of information a monitor can display.

Most monitors can detect which resolution the video card is using and then automatically switch to the appropriate setting.

Resolution is measured by the number of horizontal and vertical pixels. A pixel is the smallest element on the screen. Pixel is short for picture element.

Most monitors also let you adjust the resolution to suit your needs. To be able to change the resolution of a monitor, the video card must be able to use the same resolution.

| 640 x 480 | 800 x 600 | 1,024 x 768 | 1,280 x 1,024 | 1,600 x 1,280 |

Lower resolutions display larger images so you can see information more clearly.

Higher resolutions display smaller images so you can display more information at once.

SOUND CARD

A sound card is a circuit board that lets a computer play and record high-quality sound.

A sound card plugs into an expansion slot in a computer. Some computers do not need a sound card, since they have sound capabilities built into the system board.

A sound card is also called a sound board or audio card.

Speakers

Speakers allow you to hear the sound generated by a sound card. Most computers come equipped with low-quality speakers.

You may want to upgrade to higher quality speakers if you use your computer to play games or listen to music.

SOUND CARD APPLICATIONS

Games and Multimedia Presentations

A sound card lets you hear music, speech and sound effects during games and multimedia presentations.

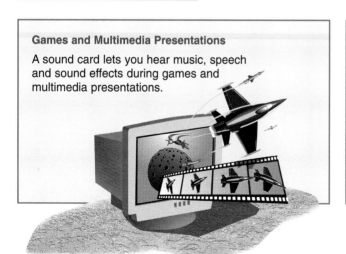

Record Sounds

You can use a sound card to record music, speech and sound effects. You can then add the sounds to documents and presentations. You can also use a sound card to compose music on your computer.

SOUND CARD CONNECTIONS

You can see the edge of a sound card at the back of a computer. A sound card has a port and several jacks where you can plug in external devices.

The edge of your sound card may look different from the sound card shown here.

Game Port

This port lets you connect a joystick or a MIDI device such as a music keyboard.

Speaker Jack

This jack lets you connect speakers or headphones to hear sound generated by a sound card.

Line Out Jack

This jack lets you connect an amplifier to play sound through your home stereo.

Microphone Jack

This jack lets you connect a microphone to record speech and other sounds.

Line In Jack

This jack lets you connect a cassette or CD player to play music.

SOUND CARD

There are several factors
to consider when choosing
a sound card.

Sampling Rate

The sampling rate of a sound
card determines the quality of
sound it can produce.

For good sound quality, buy a
sound card with a sampling
rate of at least 44.1 KHz.

If possible, listen to the
sounds produced by
various sound cards
before making your
purchase.

Full-duplex

A full-duplex sound card lets you
talk and listen at the same time.
When using a computer to have
a conversation over the Internet,
a full-duplex sound card lets
people talk at the same time.
With a half-duplex card, people
must take turns talking.

3D Sound

A sound card that offers 3D sound
capabilities produces sound that seems
to come from several directions. 3D
sound cards are useful for enhancing
the sounds in computer games and
multimedia presentations.

MIDI SUPPORT

Musical Instrument Digital Interface (MIDI) is a set of instructions that allow computers and musical devices to exchange data. This lets you connect a musical instrument, such as a synthesizer, to a computer to play, record and edit music. Many musicians use MIDI to compose music on a computer.

A sound card that supports MIDI also ensures that a computer can generate the sounds in games, multimedia CD-ROMs and presentation packages.

There are two ways a sound card can produce MIDI sound.

Wavetable Synthesis

Wavetable synthesis uses actual recordings of musical instruments and speech to produce MIDI sound. This results in rich, realistic sound. Wavetable synthesis is now available on most sound cards.

FM Synthesis

FM synthesis is an older method of producing MIDI sound. This method uses mathematical formulas to imitate the sounds of musical instruments and speech, resulting in less realistic sound. FM synthesis is available on some low-range quality sound cards.

TV TUNER CARD

A TV tuner card allows you to watch television programs on your computer.

A TV tuner card is a circuit board that plugs into an expansion slot in a computer.

TV tuner cards combine computer and television technology. This combination, or convergence, of technologies is creating an exciting new form of entertainment and communication.

Video Card

TV tuner cards require a video card to operate. Some TV tuner cards connect to the video card in your computer, but many TV tuner cards have a built-in video card.

TV TUNER CARD FEATURES

Resize

TV tuner cards can display a television program using the entire display area of a monitor or using a window that you can easily resize to suit your needs. This is useful if you want to watch a television program while performing other tasks on your computer.

Closed Captioning

Most TV tuner cards can help you find television programs of interest by scanning the closed captioning text of a television channel for a keyword you specify. When the keyword appears, the TV tuner card displays the television program on your monitor. Most TV tuner cards also allow you to save the closed captioning text from a television program as a file on your hard drive.

Intercast Technology

Some television channels use Intercast technology to broadcast additional information with their programs. This allows you to watch a television program and view text and images related to the program at the same time.

For example, when you watch a car race, you can also view information such as the average speed of a driver. Most TV tuner cards support Intercast technology.

Video Capture

Most TV tuner cards allow you to save still images and full-motion video clips from a television program as a file on your hard drive. You can then use these images and video clips in documents, e-mail messages or presentations.

MODEM

A modem lets computers exchange information through telephone lines.

A modem translates computer information into a form that can transmit over phone lines. The receiving modem translates the information it receives into a form the computer can understand.

PHONE LINE

You can use the same phone line for telephone and modem calls, but you will not be able to use the telephone and the modem at the same time. If your telephone and modem share the same line, make sure you turn off the call waiting feature when using your modem, since this feature could disrupt the modem connection.

ACCESS INFORMATION

You can use a modem to connect to the Internet so you can access information and meet people with similar interests.

When traveling or at home, you can use a modem to access information stored on the network at work. You can send and receive electronic mail (e-mail) and work with office files.

SEND AND RECEIVE FAXES

Most modems can send and receive faxes.
With a fax modem, you can create a document
on your computer and then fax the document
to another computer or fax machine.

VOICE CAPABILITIES

Some modems have voice capabilities that allow
you to use the modem to send and receive voice
telephone calls. This lets you use the modem as
a hands-free telephone. You
may also be able to use
a modem with voice
capabilities as an
answering machine
for voice telephone
messages.

TYPES OF MODEMS

Internal Modem

An internal modem is a circuit board that plugs
into an expansion slot inside a computer. An
internal modem is generally less expensive than
an external modem, but
is more difficult to set up.

External Modem

An external modem is a small box that connects
to the back of a computer. An external modem
takes up room on your desk, but you can use this
type of modem with more than one computer.

MODEM

The speed of a modem determines how fast it can send and receive information through telephone lines.

Modem speed is measured in bits per second (bps). Faster modems transfer information more quickly. This will save you time and reduce online service charges. You should buy a modem with a speed of 56,000 bps.

Modem speed is also measured in kilobits per second (Kbps). For example, a 56,000 bps modem is also referred to as a 56 Kbps modem.

Line Quality

The speed at which information transfers depends on the quality of the phone line. For example, a modem with a speed of 56 Kbps may not reach that speed if the phone line quality is poor.

Modem Standards

Modem standards ensure that modems made by different manufacturers can communicate with each other. V.90 is the current standard for 56 Kbps modems, though a new V.92 standard has been proposed. A V.90 modem can receive data at a speed of 56 Kbps but can only send data at a speed of 33.6 Kbps.

HOW MODEMS COMMUNICATE

Communications Program

A modem needs a communications program to manage the transmission of information with another modem. This type of program usually comes packaged with a modem.

Handshake

When your modem first contacts another modem, you may hear a series of squeals and signals. This is called a handshake. Just as two people shake hands to greet each other, modems perform a handshake to establish how they will exchange information.

Online

You are online when your modem has successfully connected to another modem. This means the modems are ready to exchange information. When your modem is not connected to another modem, you are offline.

DATA COMPRESSION

A modem can compress, or squeeze together, data sent to another modem to speed the transfer of data. The speed of data transfer depends on the type of file being sent. For example, a text file will compress significantly more than an image file.

When the information reaches its intended destination, the receiving modem decompresses the information.

A modem uses error control to ensure that information reliably reaches its destination.

HIGH-SPEED INTERNET CONNECTIONS

There are several types of high-speed connections that you can use to connect to the Internet instead of using a modem.

High-speed Internet connections are sometimes referred to as broadband connections.

ADVANTAGES OF HIGH-SPEED CONNECTIONS

Frees up Telephone Line

Unlike a modem, a high-speed connection does not tie up your telephone line while you are on the Internet. This allows you to make telephone calls or use a fax machine while you are connected to the Internet.

24-Hour Connection

A high-speed connection allows you to be connected to the Internet 24-hours a day. This saves you from having to dial in to your Internet service provider each time you want to connect to the Internet. This is useful when you want to continuously monitor information, such as financial news.

Fast Access

Using a high-speed connection allows you to quickly access information of interest on the Internet. For example, sound and video transfer to your computer faster, so you can watch live video on the Internet more easily.

TYPES OF HIGH-SPEED CONNECTIONS

ISDN

An Integrated Services Digital Network (ISDN) line is a digital phone line offered by telephone companies in most cities. An ISDN line can transfer information at speeds from 56 Kbps to 128 Kbps.

DSL

Digital Subscriber Line (DSL) is a high-speed digital phone line service offered by telephone companies in most cities. DSL can transfer information at speeds from 1,000 Kbps to 9,000 Kbps.

Cable Modem

A cable modem allows you to connect to the Internet with the same type of cable that attaches to a television set. A cable modem can transfer information at a speed of up to 4,000 Kbps. You can contact your local cable company to determine if they offer cable Internet service.

Emerging Technologies

Companies are constantly working on ways to send more information over the Internet at faster speeds. Some technologies that are currently emerging include using satellites and electric power lines to transfer information.

SCANNER

A scanner is a device that reads images and text into a computer.

SCAN IMAGES

You can scan images such as photographs, drawings and logos into a computer. You can then use the images in documents, such as reports or newsletters.

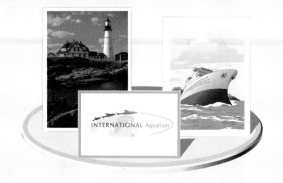

Most scanners come with image editing software, which lets you change the appearance of a scanned image.

SCAN TEXT

You can scan text to quickly enter documents into a computer. This lets you scan interesting paper documents and e-mail them to friends or colleagues. You can also scan documents to store them on your computer for quick access.

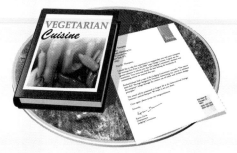

Most scanners come with Optical Character Recognition (OCR) software. This software places scanned text into a document that can be edited in a word processor.

TYPES OF SCANNERS

Flatbed Scanner

A flatbed scanner can scan single sheets of paper and pages from a book. Most flatbed scanners can scan documents that measure 8 1/2 by 11 inches. Some flatbed scanners can scan larger documents.

Sheet-fed Scanner

A sheet-fed scanner can scan only single sheets of paper. If you want to scan a page from a book, you have to tear out the page. Sheet-fed scanners are less expensive and more compact than flatbed scanners, but produce lower quality images.

Handheld Scanner

A handheld scanner usually has a scanning width of approximately four inches and is useful for copying small images such as signatures, logos and small photographs.

Smaller handheld scanners that resemble highlighter pens are also available. These scanners are useful for scanning lines of text.

SCANNER

COLOR DEPTH

The color depth of a scanner is measured in bits and indicates the number of colors the scanner can detect. The more colors the scanner can detect, the higher the quality of the scan. Scanners commonly have a 36-bit color depth.

SCANNING MODE

When scanning an image, you can choose the scanning mode. The scanning mode you choose will affect the quality of the scan and the amount of space that the scanned image takes up on your computer.

Line Art

The line art mode scans an image using black and white, creating a scanned image with a small file size.

Grayscale

The grayscale mode scans an image using black, white and shades of gray. This creates an image with a larger file size than the line art mode.

Color

The color mode scans an image using shades of red, blue and green, resulting in a scanned image with a larger file size.

RESOLUTION

The resolution of a scanner determines the amount of detail the scanner can detect. Scanner resolution is measured in dots per inch (dpi). Common scanner resolutions range from 600 dpi to 2400 dpi.

Resolution can also be expressed with two numbers (example: 600 x 1200 dpi). These numbers describe the number of dots a scanner can detect across and down one square inch.

Choose the Resolution

Scanning an image at a high resolution results in a clearer, more detailed image, but requires more scanning time and storage space.

You usually do not need to scan an image at a higher resolution than a printer can produce or a monitor can display.

20 dpi

72 dpi

300 dpi

If you plan to print an image on a 300 dpi printer, you do not need to scan at a resolution higher than 300 dpi. Most monitors have a maximum resolution of 72 dpi. If you plan to display an image on a monitor or on the Internet, you do not need to scan at a resolution higher than 72 dpi.

SPEAKERS

Speakers allow you to hear the sound generated by your computer.

Most computers come equipped with low-quality speakers. You may want to purchase higher quality speakers if you use your computer to play games or listen to music CDs.

SPEAKER CONSIDERATIONS

Speaker Systems

Speaker systems commonly have between two and five speakers. The number of speakers can affect the quality of the sound the speakers produce. For example, a speaker system that contains more than two speakers lets you take advantage of surround sound. Surround sound directs sound to different speakers so that the sound comes from multiple directions.

Frequency

Frequency is measured in hertz (Hz) and refers to the range of high and low sounds speakers can produce. The range of human hearing is 20 Hz to 20,000 Hz. Some high-quality speakers have a frequency of 40 Hz to 20,000 Hz.

Shielded Speakers

When choosing speakers, make sure you select shielded speakers. Shielded speakers prevent the magnets inside the speakers from distorting the images on a monitor.

Digital Speakers

Digital speakers can play sound received in digital format. This allows digital speakers to produce higher quality sound than analog speakers, which can only work with sound that has already been converted to analog format by a computer.

Some digital speakers are designed to work with specific sound cards. Other digital speakers plug into a USB port and do not need a sound card. This allows your computer to send sound directly to the speakers.

Additional Features

Some speakers include additional features that can enhance the quality of sound the speakers produce. For example, a built-in amplifier can strengthen the signal from a computer to improve speaker performance. Speakers that use 3D sound technology seem to produce sound from a wider area. Some speaker systems also include a subwoofer, which produces low-frequency sounds and gives the speakers a richer sound.

USB PORT

A Universal Serial Bus (USB) port is a connector you can use to attach external devices to your computer.

Most new computers come with two USB ports. If your computer does not have a USB port, you can purchase a USB expansion card to add a USB port to the computer.

USB-COMPATIBLE DEVICES

A device must be USB-compatible to connect to a USB port. A wide variety of devices, such as printers, scanners, joysticks, digital cameras and speakers, are now available in USB-compatible versions. You can check the documentation for a device to determine if the device is USB-compatible.

SPEED

The current version of USB can transfer information at a speed of up to 12 megabits per second (Mbps). A new version of USB, called USB 2.0 or USB2, is currently in production. USB 2.0 will be able to transfer information at a speed of up to 480 Mbps.

PLUG AND PLAY

USB ports use Plug and Play technology. This means that when you plug a device into a USB port, your computer can automatically detect and set up the device for you.

HOT PLUG

A USB port allows you to add and remove devices without having to turn off your computer. This is known as hot plugging, or hot swapping. Your computer will automatically detect when a device is added or removed.

CONNECT MULTIPLE DEVICES

A USB port can support up to 127 devices. This allows you to connect multiple devices using the same USB port.

USB Hub

You can use a USB hub to connect multiple devices to a USB port. A USB hub is a device that provides additional ports. USB hubs typically have four or more USB ports.

Daisy Chain

Some USB devices have built-in USB ports that you can use to plug in other devices. This allows you to create a chain of devices that you can connect to a single USB port on your computer. This method of connecting devices is known as daisy chaining.

FIREWIRE PORT

A FireWire port is a high-speed connector that allows information to quickly transfer between a computer and an external device.

FireWire is also known as IEEE 1394 or i.LINK.

Some new computers come with two or more FireWire ports. If your computer does not have a FireWire port, you can purchase a FireWire expansion card.

CONNECT MULTIPLE DEVICES

A FireWire port can support up to 63 devices. This lets you connect multiple devices, such as a digital camera, digital video camera and external hard drive using the same FireWire port.

Daisy Chain

Some FireWire devices have built-in FireWire ports that you can use to plug in other devices. This allows you to create a chain of devices that you can connect to a single FireWire port on your computer. This method of connecting devices is called daisy chaining.

SPEED

A FireWire port can transfer information at a speed of up to 400 megabits per second (Mbps). This makes a FireWire port useful for connecting high-speed devices such as digital video cameras and external hard drives.

FIREWIRE-COMPATIBLE DEVICES

A device must be FireWire-compatible to connect to a FireWire port. You can check the documentation for a device to determine if the device is FireWire-compatible.

PLUG AND PLAY

FireWire ports use Plug and Play technology. When you plug a device into a FireWire port, your computer can automatically detect and set up the device for you. This allows you to easily connect new devices to your computer.

HOT PLUG

FireWire ports allow you to add and remove devices without having to turn off your computer. This is called hot plugging, or hot swapping. Your computer will automatically detect when a device is added or removed.

CHAPTER 3

Processing

Wondering how a computer processes information? Find out how in this chapter.

MEMORY

Memory, also called Random Access Memory (RAM), temporarily stores data inside a computer.

Memory works like a blackboard that is constantly overwritten with new data. The data stored in memory disappears when you turn off the computer.

MEMORY SIZE

The amount of memory determines the number of programs a computer can run at once and how fast programs will operate.

Memory is measured in megabytes (MB). You should buy a computer with at least 64 MB of memory.

You can improve the performance of a computer by adding more memory. The capabilities of your system board may limit the amount of memory you can add.

ACCESS SPEED

The speed at which information is stored and accessed in memory is called access speed. Access speed is usually measured in megahertz (MHz). When adding memory to your computer, make sure the access speed of the memory is compatible with the speed of the system board. Most system boards can support memory with an access speed of 100 MHz.

MEMORY CHIPS

Dynamic RAM (DRAM) is a type of memory chip that makes up the main memory in many computer systems.

Synchronous DRAM (SDRAM) is a faster type of memory chip found in most new computer systems. Many computers can use both DRAM and SDRAM memory chips.

Rambus DRAM (RDRAM) is a new type of memory chip often found in high-performance computers.

Memory Module

A memory module is a circuit board that holds memory chips. A Single In-line Memory Module (SIMM) holds up to nine memory chips. New computers also accept Dual In-line Memory Modules (DIMMs), which can hold up to 18 memory chips. You can add more memory to a computer by inserting additional memory modules.

Memory Module Socket

A memory module socket is a socket on the system board where you plug in a memory module.

VIRTUAL MEMORY

If you have limited memory or you have many programs open, your computer may need to use part of the hard drive to simulate more memory.

This simulated memory is called virtual memory and allows the computer to continue operating, but at a much slower speed.

ROM

Unlike RAM, Read-Only Memory (ROM) is permanent and cannot be changed. ROM stores instructions that help prepare the computer for use each time you turn on the computer.

CPU

The Central Processing Unit (CPU) is the main chip in a computer.

The CPU processes instructions, performs calculations and manages the flow of information through a computer system. The CPU performs millions of calculations every second.

The CPU is also called the microprocessor or processor.

CPU COMPLEXITY

Imagine a road map of the United States printed on a fingernail and you can imagine the complexity of a CPU. The elements in a CPU can be as small as 0.18 microns wide. By comparison, a human hair is approximately 100 microns wide.

The manufacturing plants that produce CPUs must be many times cleaner than hospital operating rooms. Ultra-sensitive dust filtering systems are needed to eliminate particles that could damage the CPUs during production.

CHOOSE A CPU

There are several factors that determine the performance of a CPU.

Manufacturer

The most popular CPUs for personal computers are made by Intel. Other popular CPU manufacturers include AMD and VIA Technologies.

Generation

Each new generation of CPU is more powerful than the one before. Newer CPUs can process more instructions at a time. For example, a newer generation CPU such as the Intel Pentium 4 is more powerful than an older CPU such as the Intel Pentium III.

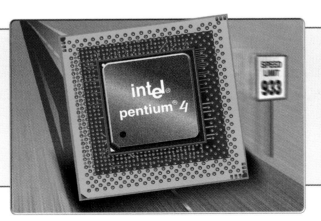

Speed

Each type of CPU is available in several speeds. The CPU speed is a major factor in determining how fast a computer operates. The faster the speed, the faster the computer operates.

The speed of a CPU is commonly measured in megahertz (MHz), or millions of cycles per second. New, faster CPUs are now measured in gigahertz (GHz), or billions of cycles per second.

TYPES OF CPUs

Intel Pentium Processor

Pentium is a popular type of CPU manufactured by Intel. There are several generations of Intel Pentium CPUs, including Pentium, Pentium II, Pentium III and Pentium 4. Intel Pentium 4 is the most recent generation, with a processing speed of over 1 GHz.

Intel Pentium III CPUs are still found in many new computers, while the older Pentium II and Pentium generations are now less common. Intel Pentium III CPUs are available with speeds such as 933 MHz and 1.13 GHz.

Intel Celeron Processor

Intel's Celeron CPU is an inexpensive CPU designed to meet the needs and budgets of most home computer users. Intel Celeron CPUs are similar to Intel Pentium II CPUs, but have less built-in memory. Intel Celeron CPUs are available with speeds such as 600 MHz and 700 MHz.

AMD Athlon Processor

The AMD Athlon CPU is a high-performance processor manufactured by AMD. This CPU is suitable for businesses and home computer users who want a powerful processor.

AMD Athlon CPUs are available with speeds such as 1.1 GHz and 1.2 GHz.

AMD Duron Processor

AMD manufactures the AMD Duron CPU, which is an inexpensive CPU that meets the needs of most home computer users. AMD Duron CPUs offer relatively high speeds at a low cost.

AMD Duron CPUs are available with speeds such as 750 MHz and 800 MHz.

VIA Cyrix Processor

Cyrix is a type of CPU manufactured by VIA Technologies. VIA Cyrix CPUs are available in two generations–VIA Cyrix MII and VIA Cyrix III. These CPUs are designed for businesses and home computer users who want an inexpensive CPU with good quality processing capabilities.

The VIA Cyrix MII is available with speeds such as 400 MHz and 433 MHz. The VIA Cyrix III is available with speeds such as 550 MHz and 600 MHz.

MEMORY CACHE

Memory cache speeds up a computer by storing data the computer has recently used.

RAM (Main Memory)

Internal Cache

External Cache

There are two types of memory cache–internal cache and external cache.

INTERNAL CACHE

When a computer needs data, the computer first looks in the internal cache. Internal cache is on the CPU chip and provides the fastest way for the computer to get data. Internal cache is also called L1 or primary cache.

EXTERNAL CACHE

If the computer cannot find the data it needs in the internal cache, the computer looks in the external cache. External cache is usually on the system board and consists of Static RAM (SRAM) chips.

Accessing external cache is generally slower than internal cache, but is much faster than retrieving data from RAM. In some computers, the external cache is built into the CPU chip, which makes accessing the cache much faster.

RAM

If the computer cannot find the data it needs in the internal or external cache, the computer must get the data from the slower main memory, called RAM.

Each time the computer requests data from RAM, the computer places a copy of the data in the memory cache. This process constantly updates the memory cache so it always contains the most recently used data.

USING MEMORY CACHE

Using memory cache is similar to working with documents in your office. When you need information, you look for information in a specific order. Each step along the way takes up more of your valuable time.

❶ Look through documents on your desk (internal cache).

❷ Look through documents in your desk drawer (external cache).

❸ Look through documents in your filing cabinet (RAM).

Working without memory cache would be similar to looking through the filing cabinet each time you need a document.

BUS

The bus is the electronic pathway that carries information between devices in a computer.

BUS WIDTH

The bus width is similar to the number of lanes on a highway. The greater the width, the more data can flow along the bus at a time. Bus width is measured in bits. Eight bits equals one character.

BUS SPEED

The bus speed is similar to the speed limit on a highway. The higher the speed, the faster data travels along the bus. Bus speed is measured in megahertz (MHz), or millions of cycles per second.

BUS TYPES

ISA Bus

The Industry Standard Architecture (ISA) bus is the slowest and oldest type of bus. This bus is often used for transferring information to and from a slow device, such as a modem. The ISA bus has a width of 16 bits and a speed of 8 MHz.

The ISA bus is commonly found in Pentium and Pentium II computers.

PCI Bus

The Peripheral Component Interconnect (PCI) bus is a sophisticated type of bus found in new computers. This bus can handle many high-speed devices. The PCI bus can have a width of 32 or 64 bits and a speed of 33 MHz.

The PCI bus supports Plug and Play, which lets you add new devices to a computer without complex installation procedures.

The PCI bus is commonly found in Pentium II, Pentium III and Pentium 4 computers.

AGP Bus

An Accelerated Graphics Port (AGP) bus is specifically designed to carry complex graphics data between an AGP video card and your computer's main memory. The AGP bus has a width of 32 bits and a speed of 66 MHz.

The AGP bus is found in Pentium II, Pentium III and Pentium 4 computers.

Storage Devices

What is a hard drive? What does a CD-RW drive do? Learn about storage devices in this chapter.

HARD DRIVE

The hard drive is the primary device that a computer uses to store information.

■ Most computers have one hard drive, located inside the computer case.

■ The hard drive light is on when the computer is using the hard drive. Do not move the computer when this light is on.

The hard drive is also called the hard disk, hard disk drive or fixed disk drive.

Some hard drives, called external hard drives, are located outside the computer case and plug into the back of a computer.

Inside a Hard Drive

The hard drive magnetically stores data on a stack of rotating disks, called platters.

■ A hard drive has several read/write heads that read and record data on the disks.

HARD DRIVE CONTENTS

Program Files

A hard drive stores your operating system and programs. When you buy a new program, you must install, or copy, the program files to your hard drive before you can use the program.

Programs come on a CD-ROM disc, DVD-ROM disc or several floppy disks.

Data Files

A hard drive stores your data files, such as documents, spreadsheets and images.

STORE FILES

Save Files

When you are creating a document, the computer stores the document in temporary memory. If you want to store a document for future use, you can save the document to the hard drive. If you do not save the document, the document will be lost when there is a power failure or you turn off the computer.

File System

The file system determines how information is stored on a hard drive. The file system your computer uses depends on the operating system you are using and how the computer is set up. Common file systems include FAT, FAT32 and NTFS.

CHOOSE A HARD DRIVE

Capacity

The amount of information a hard drive can store is measured in bytes.

A hard drive with a capacity of 10 to 20 GB will suit most home and business users.

Purchase the largest hard drive you can afford. New programs and data will quickly fill a hard drive. For example, Microsoft Office requires about 250 MB of hard drive space. The Windows Me operating system requires about 300 MB.

Speed

The speed at which the platters in the hard drive spin is measured in Revolutions Per Minute (RPM). The higher the RPM, the faster the hard drive can find and record data on the platters.

The speed at which a hard drive finds data is referred to as the average access time. Average access time is measured in milliseconds (ms). One millisecond equals 1/1000 of a second. Most hard drives have an average access time of 5 to 15 ms. The lower the average access time, the faster the hard drive.

CONNECTION TYPE

EIDE

Enhanced Integrated Drive Electronics (EIDE) is a fast way to connect a hard drive and other devices to a computer. Most computers come with an EIDE connection. EIDE is often referred to as IDE.

EIDE can support a total of four devices, including hard drives, CD-ROM drives, DVD-ROM drives and tape drives.

Ultra Direct Memory Access (UDMA) is an enhancement to EIDE that increases the speed at which data transfers over an EIDE connection.

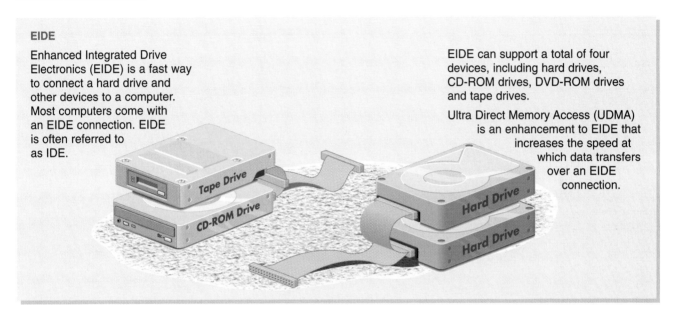

SCSI

Small Computer System Interface (SCSI, pronounced "scuzzy") is the fastest, most flexible, but most expensive way to connect a hard drive and other devices to a computer.

The most common type of SCSI can connect up to seven devices, including removable drives, CD-ROM drives, DVD-ROM drives, tape drives and scanners. There are also other types of SCSI available that transmit data faster and connect more devices.

DISK CACHE

The disk cache speeds up the computer by storing data the computer has recently used.

■ The disk cache is an area of memory where the computer stores recently used data.

When the computer needs data, the computer first looks in the disk cache. The disk cache can supply data thousands of times faster than the hard drive.

If the computer cannot find the data it needs in the disk cache, the computer looks on the hard drive.

HARD DRIVE

DISK CACHE

Each time the computer requests data from the hard drive, the computer places a copy of the data in the disk cache. This process constantly updates the disk cache so it always contains the most recently used data.

PROTECT A HARD DRIVE

Virus

A virus is a program that disrupts the normal operation of a computer. A virus can cause a variety of problems, such as the appearance of annoying messages on the screen or the destruction of information on the hard drive.

Files you receive on a floppy disk or from the Internet may contain viruses. You should use a virus scanner program to regularly check your computer for viruses.

Back Up Data

You should copy the files stored on your hard drive to removable disks or tape cartridges. This provides extra copies in case the original files are lost or damaged due to viruses or computer failure.

You do not need to back up the programs stored on your computer if you have the original program disc or disks. If a program on your hard drive is lost or damaged, you can use the original disc or disks to re-install the program at any time.

OPTIMIZE A HARD DRIVE

Defragment a Drive

A fragmented hard drive stores parts of a file in many different locations. To retrieve a file, the computer must search many areas of the drive.

You can use a defragmentation program to place all parts of a file in one location. This reduces the time the hard drive spends locating the file.

Defragmenting your hard drive once a month can improve the performance of the computer. Most operating systems include a defragmentation program.

Repair a Drive

You can improve the performance of a computer by using a disk repair program to search for and repair disk errors. You should check a hard drive for errors at least once a month.

Most operating systems include a disk repair program.

CREATE MORE DISK SPACE

Archive Information

Store old or rarely used files on a tape cartridge or a removable disk. You can then remove the files from your computer to provide more storage space.

Disk Cleanup

You can use a disk cleanup program to find and remove files that are no longer needed on your computer, such as temporary files. Removing unneeded files will free up space on a hard drive.

Many operating systems include a disk cleanup program.

Data Compression

You can compress, or squeeze together, the files stored on a hard drive. This can double the amount of information the drive can store.

You should only compress a hard drive if it is running out of space to store new information and you have tried all other ways of increasing the available storage space.

Most operating systems include a data compression program.

FLOPPY DRIVE

A floppy drive stores and retrieves information on floppy disks. A floppy disk is a removable device that magnetically stores data.

Most computers have a floppy drive, called drive A.

INSIDE A FLOPPY DRIVE

Floppy drives use 3.5 inch floppy disks. Inside a floppy disk is a thin, plastic, flexible disk that magnetically records data. The word floppy refers to this flexible disk.

When you insert a floppy disk into a floppy drive, the flexible disk inside the floppy disk spins. The floppy drive has read/write heads that move across the flexible disk to read and record data on the disk.

FORMATTED FLOPPY DISK

A floppy disk must be formatted before you can use it to store data. Formatting a disk prepares the disk for use by dividing it into tracks and sectors. This organizes the disk so the computer can store and retrieve data.

FLOPPY DRIVE APPLICATIONS

Transfer Data

Floppy disks are commonly used to transfer data from one computer to another. This lets you give data to friends and colleagues.

Back Up Files

You can copy important files to floppy disks. The disks will serve as backup copies if your hard drive fails or if you accidentally erase the files.

PROTECT A FLOPPY DISK

You can prevent erasing and recording information on a floppy disk by sliding the tab to the write-protected position.

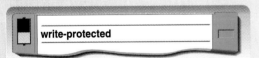

You **cannot** erase and record information.

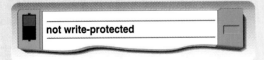

You **can** erase and record information.

Make sure you keep floppy disks away from magnets, which can damage the information stored on the disks. Also make sure you do not store floppy disks in extremely hot or cold locations and do not spill liquids such as coffee or soda on the disks.

CD-ROM DRIVE

A CD-ROM drive is a device that reads information stored on Compact Discs (CDs).

Most CD-ROM drives are located inside the computer case. External CD-ROM drives that connect to the computer by a cable are also available.

CD-ROM DISC

A CD-ROM disc is the same type of disc you buy at a music store.

A single CD-ROM disc can store up to 650 MB of data. This is equal to an entire set of encyclopedias or over 400 floppy disks. The large storage capacity of CD-ROM discs provide more room for storing large images, animation and video.

CD-ROM stands for Compact Disc-Read-Only Memory. Read-only means you cannot change the information stored on a disc.

CD-ROM APPLICATIONS

Install Programs

The large storage capacity of a CD-ROM disc makes installing new programs on your computer easy. A program that requires 20 floppy disks can easily fit on a single CD-ROM disc.

Play Multimedia CD-ROM Discs

A CD-ROM disc can store multimedia presentations. Multimedia refers to the combination of text, images, sound, animation and video. Multimedia provides a powerful way of communicating information.

There are thousands of multimedia CD-ROM discs available to inform and entertain you. You can buy multimedia CD-ROM discs at most computer stores.

Play Music CDs

You can play music CDs on a CD-ROM drive while you work. Some music CDs, called Enhanced CDs, also contain multimedia you can view on your computer. For example, an Enhanced CD can include song lyrics, artist interviews and music videos.

CD-ROM DRIVE

The speed of a CD-ROM drive determines how fast a disc spins. With faster speeds, information can transfer from a disc to the computer more quickly, which results in better performance.

The speed of a CD-ROM drive is called the data transfer rate, or throughput, and is measured in Kilobytes per second (KB/s).

CD-ROM drive speed is very important when viewing video and animation often found in games and encyclopedias. Slow speeds will result in jerky playback.

CD-ROM DRIVE SPEED	MAXIMUM DATA TRANSFER RATE
Eight (8X)	1,200 KB/s
Ten (10X)	1,600 KB/s
Twelve (12X)	1,800 KB/s
Sixteen (16X)	2,400 KB/s
Twenty-Four (24X)	3,600 KB/s
Thirty-Two (32X)	4,800 KB/s
Forty (40X)	6,000 KB/s
Forty-Eight (48X)	7,200 KB/s
Sixty (60X)	9,000 KB/s

The chart to the left displays the most common speeds available. You should buy at least a 24X CD-ROM drive.

WORK WITH A CD-ROM DISC

Insert a Disc

Most CD-ROM drives have a tray you use to insert a CD-ROM disc.

■ To insert or remove a disc, press this button.

■ The tray slides out. Place the disc, label side up, on the tray. To close the tray, press the button again.

A light is on when the CD-ROM drive is accessing information on the disc. Do not remove the disc or move the computer when this light is on.

Some CD-ROM drives do not have a tray. Instead, you slide the disc, label side up, into a slot in the CD-ROM drive.

Headphones

You can use headphones to listen to recorded sounds on a disc. Headphones are useful in noisy environments or when you want to listen to a disc privately.

Handle a Disc

When handling a CD-ROM disc, hold the disc around the edges.

Protect a Disc

When you finish using a disc, make sure you place the disc back in its protective case. Do not stack discs on top of each other.

CD-R AND CD-RW DRIVES

CD-R and CD-RW drives are devices that allow you to store information on Compact Discs (CDs).

CD-R and CD-RW drives can also play CD-ROM discs and music CDs.

CD-R DRIVE

A CD-R (Compact Disc-Recordable) drive allows you to permanently store data on a CD-R disc. CD-R discs are not erasable, so the data you record cannot be changed.

CD-RW DRIVE

A CD-RW (Compact Disc-ReWritable) drive allows you to record data on CD-RW discs. You can change the data you record on a CD-RW disc many times.

A CD-RW drive can also play and record data on CD-R discs. You can only record data on a CD-R disc once.

DRIVE SPEED

CD-R and CD-RW drives operate at several different speeds. The write speed refers to how fast a CD-R or CD-RW drive can record data onto a CD-R disc. The rewrite speed refers to how fast a CD-RW drive can record data onto a CD-RW disc. The read speed refers to how fast data transfers from a disc to the computer.

Common Drive Speeds

	CD-R	CD-RW
Write	12X	12X
Rewrite	N/A	10X
Read	24X	32X

Write Speed — Rewrite Speed — Read Speed

SOFTWARE

CD-R and CD-RW drives require special software to record data onto a disc. Most CD-R and CD-RW drives come with software specifically designed for use with the drives. You can also purchase software that provides more features, such as audio utilities to improve the quality of sound you record.

APPLICATIONS

Store and Transfer Data

CD-R and CD-RW drives commonly allow you to store up to 650 MB of data on a single disc. This lets you easily transfer data, such as software applications or multimedia presentations, between computers. Storing data on CD-R and CD-RW discs is often referred to as "burning" a CD.

Record Music

CD-R and CD-RW drives let you record music CDs. You can find music on the Internet or connect a CD player or stereo system to your computer to record music. A single CD-R or CD-RW disc can usually store up to 74 minutes of music. CD-RW discs you record may not play in some CD-R and CD-ROM drives or in some CD players.

DVD-ROM DRIVE

A DVD-ROM drive is a device that reads information stored on DVD-ROM discs.

DVD-ROM stands for Digital Versatile Disc-Read-Only Memory. Read-only means you cannot change the information stored on a disc.

A DVD-ROM disc is similar in size and shape to a CD-ROM disc, but can store a lot more information.

DVD-ROM APPLICATIONS

Multimedia

You can use a DVD-ROM drive to play multimedia DVD-ROM discs and CD-ROM discs, as well as music CDs. Most DVD-ROM drives can also play CD-R and CD-RW discs.

DVD-Video

DVD-ROM drives can play DVD-Video discs, which hold full-length, full-screen movies with much better quality than videocassettes. Many DVD-Video discs allow you to change the way you view the movie, such as displaying subtitles.

You may need special hardware, such as an MPEG-2 video decoder card, for the best playback of DVD-Video discs.

DVD CONSIDERATIONS

DVD Disc Storage Capacity

A single DVD disc can store at least 4.7 GB of data, which equals over seven CD-ROM discs.

DVD DISC	1 side/ 1 layer	1 side/ 2 layers	2 sides/ 1 layer	2 sides/ 2 layers
Storage	4.7 GB	8.5 GB	9.4 GB	17 GB

Unlike a CD-ROM disc, a DVD disc can be single-sided or double-sided. Each side can store one or two layers of data.

DVD-ROM Drive Speed

The speed of a DVD-ROM drive determines how quickly data can transfer from a disc to the computer. Currently, DVD-ROM drives can have a speed of up to 16X.

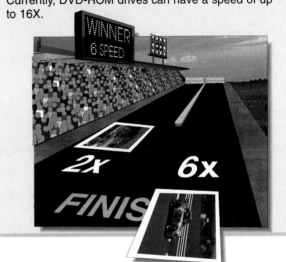

RECORDABLE DVD DRIVE

A recordable DVD drive allows you to record data on recordable DVD discs. Many recordable DVD drives are rewritable, which means that you can change the data recorded on discs. Rewritable DVD drives are commonly called DVD-RAM drives. Most recordable DVD drives can also play CD-ROM, CD-R and CD-RW discs, as well as music CDs.

REMOVABLE STORAGE DEVICE

A removable storage device allows you to store large amounts of data on removable disks.

A removable disk is similar in size and shape to a floppy disk, but can store much more data.

REMOVABLE STORAGE DEVICE APPLICATIONS

Archive Data

You can use a removable storage device to store old or rarely used files. You can then remove the files from your computer to provide more storage space.

Protect Data

You can use a removable storage device to store confidential data or backup copies of data. You can then protect the data by placing the disks in a safe place on nights and weekends.

Transfer Data

You can use a removable storage device to transfer large amounts of data between computers. For example, you can take work home or transfer data to a colleague.

When using a removable storage device to transfer data, make sure the person receiving the data uses the same type of device. Most removable storage devices cannot use disks from a different type of device.

TYPES OF REMOVABLE STORAGE DEVICES

Jaz Drive

Jaz drives are one of the most popular types of removable storage device. Jaz drives are very fast and use disks with a large storage capacity. Some Jaz drives can store up to 2 GB of data on a single disk.

Zip Drive

Zip drives are currently a very popular type of removable storage device. A Zip drive is relatively inexpensive and can store up to 250 MB of data on a single disk.

ORB Drive

ORB drives are fast removable storage devices that are available at an affordable price. An ORB drive can store up to 2.2 GB of data on a single disk, which is currently the largest storage capacity of all removable disks.

LS-120 Drive

An LS-120 drive can store up to 120 MB of data on a single disk. Unlike many other removable storage devices, LS-120 drives also accept regular floppy disks.

REMOVABLE STORAGE DEVICE

Speed

Each removable storage device stores and accesses data at a specific speed. The type of device and how the device connects to the computer determines the speed.

Software

Removable storage devices usually include a variety of software that lets you use the device. For example, a removable storage device may come with software that allows you to back up data on your computer, copy the contents of disks or restore data after a computer failure.

Internal or External

An internal removable storage device is located inside the computer case. An internal removable storage device is more difficult to set up than an external removable storage device.

An external removable storage device connects to a computer by a cable. An external removable storage device takes up room on your desk, but can easily be used with more than one computer.

REMOVABLE DISKS

Disk Capacity

The amount of data a removable disk can store is measured in bytes. Some removable disks can store up to 2.2 GB, while others store as little as 120 MB. A large disk capacity is useful for storing large files, such as images or videos.

Types of Disks

Some removable disks contain a thin, flexible disk, similar to the media used in floppy disks. Other removable disks contain hard platters, similar to the media used in hard drives. Disks containing hard platters are usually faster and store more data than disks containing flexible media.

Protect a Removable Disk

The data on a removable disk can be damaged if the disk is mishandled or exposed to magnetic fields. To avoid damage, store disks in a cool, dry, clean environment, away from the magnetic fields generated by your monitor and speakers.

TAPE DRIVE

A tape drive stores and retrieves information on tape cartridges.

A tape drive can be inside the computer case or connected to the computer by a cable. An external tape drive is more expensive, but can be used with more than one computer.

Tape cartridges are similar to the cassettes you buy at music stores. You should store tape cartridges in a cool, dry place, away from electrical equipment.

TYPES OF TAPE DRIVES

Travan Drive

Travan drives are the most common type of tape drive. There are several levels of Travan drives and tape cartridges, including TR-1, TR-2, TR-3, TR-4 and TR-5. The higher the level, the more data the drive or tape cartridge can store. A high-quality Travan drive can store up to 10 GB of data on a single Travan cartridge.

DAT Drive

A Digital Audio Tape (DAT) drive is faster than a Travan drive, but is more expensive. A high-quality DAT drive can store up to 24 GB of data on a single DAT cartridge.

TAPE DRIVE APPLICATIONS

Archive Data

You can copy old or rarely used files from your computer to tape cartridges. You can then remove the files from your computer to provide more storage space.

Transfer Data

You can use a tape drive to transfer large amounts of information between computers. Make sure the person receiving the data uses the same type of tape drive.

Back Up Data

Most people use tape drives to make backup copies of files stored on a computer. This provides extra copies in case the original files are lost or damaged due to viruses or computer failure.

BACKUP PROGRAM

A backup program helps you copy the files stored on your computer to tape cartridges. Most tape drives come with a backup program specifically designed for use with the tape drive. Many operating systems also include a backup program.

A backup program can compress, or squeeze together, data you are backing up. This may allow you to double the amount of data you can store on a tape cartridge.

CHAPTER 5

Software

Ready to start that report? Browse through this chapter to discover how software can help you get the job done.

Game Software

New Enhanced Sound

D GRAPHICS!

INTRODUCTION TO SOFTWARE

Software helps you accomplish specific tasks.

You can use software to write letters, manage your finances, draw pictures, play games and much more.

Software is also called an application or a program.

GET SOFTWARE

You can buy software at computer stores. There are also thousands of programs available on the Internet.

INSTALL SOFTWARE

Software you buy at a computer store may come on a CD-ROM disc, a DVD-ROM disc or several floppy disks. Before you can use the software, you install, or copy, the contents of the disc or disks onto your computer. Using a CD-ROM or DVD-ROM disc is a fast method of installing software.

SOFTWARE UPDATES

New Version

When a manufacturer adds new features to existing software, the updated software is given a new name or new version number. This helps people distinguish new versions of the software from older versions.

Patch

Manufacturers may also create minor software updates, called patches, to make corrections or improvements to software. You can often find a patch on the software manufacturer's Web site. A patch is also referred to as a service pack.

BUNDLED SOFTWARE

Bundled software is software that comes with a new computer system or device, such as a printer. Companies often include bundled software to let you start using the new equipment right away. For example, new computer systems usually come with word processing, spreadsheet and graphics programs.

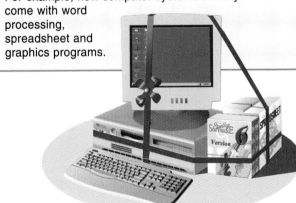

GET HELP

Most software comes with a built-in help feature and printed documentation to help you learn to use the software. You can also buy computer books that contain detailed, step-by-step instructions or visit the manufacturer's Web site for more information about the software.

WORD PROCESSOR

A word processor helps you create professional-looking documents quickly and efficiently.

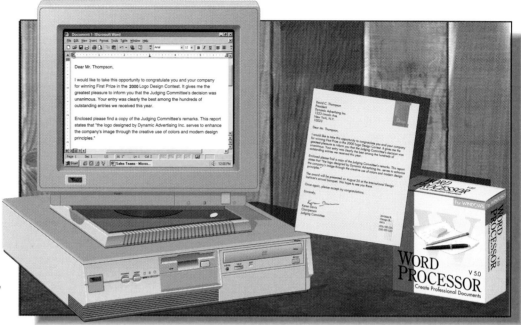

Commonly used word processing programs include Microsoft Word, Corel WordPerfect and Lotus Word Pro.

WORD PROCESSING HIGHLIGHTS

Documents

You can create many different types of documents, such as letters, reports, manuals, newsletters, brochures and Web pages.

Tables

You can create a table to neatly organize the information in a document. You can enhance the appearance of a table by adding colors and borders to the table.

Mail Merge

Most Word processors offer a mail merge feature that lets you quickly produce personalized letters, envelopes and mailing labels for each person on a mailing list.

WORD PROCESSING BASICS

Insertion Point

The flashing line on a screen is called the insertion point. The insertion point indicates where the text you type will appear.

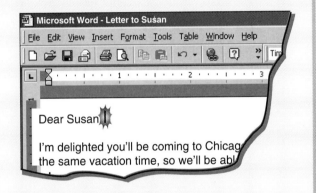

Word Wrap

When the text you type reaches the end of a line, a word processor automatically moves the text to the next line. This is called word wrapping. When typing text, you need to press the **Enter** key only when you want to start a new paragraph.

When you use a word processor to type a letter, the text automatically wraps to the next line as you type.

Scroll

If you create a long document, the computer screen cannot display all the text at the same time. You must scroll up or down to view and edit other parts of the document.

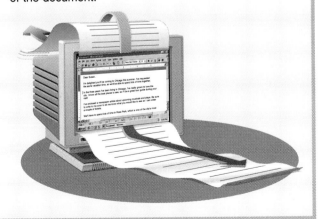

Print

You can produce a paper copy of a document. Word processors let you see on the screen exactly what a printed document will look like.

WORD PROCESSOR

EDIT A DOCUMENT

Edit Text

After typing text in a document, you can easily add, delete or move text. A word processor also remembers the last changes you made to a document and lets you undo the changes.

Thesaurus

Many word processors include a thesaurus that lets you replace a word in a document with one that is more suitable.

Spelling and Grammar

A word processor includes a spell checker you can use to find and correct spelling errors in a document. Some word processors correct common spelling errors as you type.

Most word processors also include a grammar checker you can use to check a document for grammar, punctuation and stylistic errors.

Find and Replace

You can find and replace every occurrence of a word or phrase in a document. This is useful if you have frequently misspelled a name.

ENHANCE A DOCUMENT

Font

Word processors include a variety of fonts you can use to create attractive documents. You can enhance the appearance of a document by changing the font, size or style of the text.

Images

Most word processors include many types of images that you can use to enhance the appearance of a document. Using images can help you draw attention to important information.

Paragraph Formatting

Word processors have many features you can use to enhance the appearance of paragraphs in a document. For example, you can change the line spacing, align text in different ways and create bulleted or numbered lists.

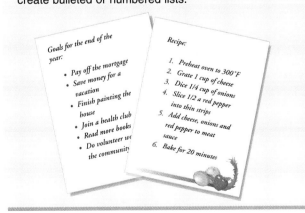

Page Formatting

Word processors also provide features that allow you to enhance the overall appearance of the pages in a document. For example, you can change the margin settings, add page numbers and create page borders.

SPREADSHEET

A spreadsheet program helps you manage personal and business finances.

Commonly used spreadsheet programs include Microsoft Excel, Corel Quattro Pro and Lotus 1-2-3.

SPREADSHEET APPLICATIONS

Manage Finances

You can use a spreadsheet program to perform calculations, analyze data and present information.

Manage Data in a List

A spreadsheet program lets you store a large collection of information, such as a mailing or product list. Spreadsheet programs include tools for organizing, managing, sorting and retrieving data.

If you want greater control over a list stored on your computer, use a database program. Database programs are specifically designed to manage lists of data.

SPREADSHEET BASICS

A spreadsheet consists of columns, rows and cells.

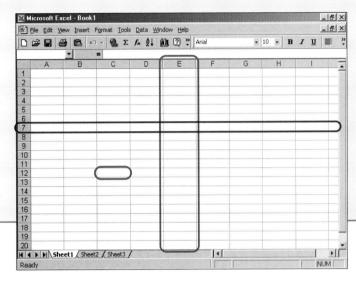

Column

A column is a vertical line of cells. A letter identifies each column (example: E).

Row

A row is a horizontal line of cells. A number identifies each row (example: 7).

Cell

A cell is one box in a spreadsheet. You enter information into the cells in a spreadsheet.

Cell Reference

A cell reference, or cell address, defines the location of each cell in a spreadsheet. A cell reference consists of a column letter followed by a row number (example: B3).

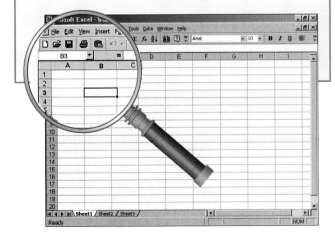

Work With Rows and Columns

You can change the width of columns and the height of rows to better fit the data in a spreadsheet. You can also insert rows and columns into a spreadsheet to add new data or delete rows and columns to remove data you no longer need.

SPREADSHEET

EDIT A SPREADSHEET

Edit Data

After entering data in a spreadsheet, you can add, delete, move and copy the data. Most spreadsheet programs can remember the last change you made and let you undo, or cancel, the change.

Complete a Series

A spreadsheet program can save you time by completing a series of numbers, text or time periods for you. You can complete a series across a row or down a column in a spreadsheet.

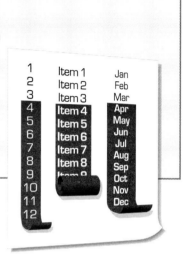

ENHANCE A SPREADSHEET

Format Data

You can easily change the font of data in a spreadsheet to make the spreadsheet more appealing. You can also change the size and alignment of data to make the data easier to read and identify.

Format a Spreadsheet

A spreadsheet program offers many features that help you enhance the overall appearance of a spreadsheet. For example, you can add borders, shading and color to cells.

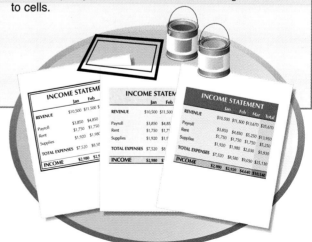

FORMULAS AND FUNCTIONS

Formula

A formula helps you calculate and analyze data in a spreadsheet. If you change a number used in a formula, you do not have to manually redo all the calculations. A spreadsheet program will automatically redo the calculations and display the new results.

Function

A function is a ready-to-use formula that helps you perform specialized calculations. For example, the SUM function adds a list of numbers. The AVERAGE function calculates the average value of a list of numbers.

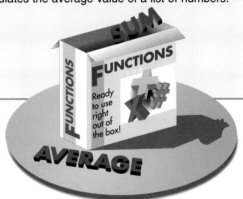

CHART

Spreadsheet programs let you create charts to graphically display the data in a spreadsheet. After creating a chart, you can select a different type of chart that will better suit the data.

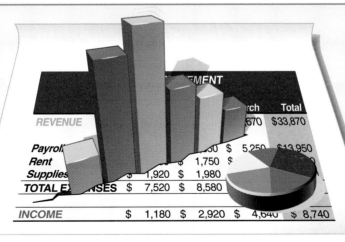

If you later change the data used in a chart, the spreadsheet program will automatically update the chart for you.

DATABASE

A database program helps you manage large collections of information.

Database programs are commonly used to manage mailing lists, phone directories, product listings and payroll information.

Commonly used database programs include Microsoft Access, Corel Paradox and Lotus Approach.

DATABASE APPLICATIONS

Store Information

You can use a database program to keep large collections of information organized and up-to-date.

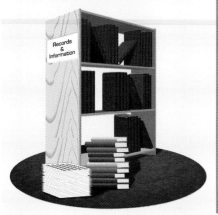

Analyze Information

You can perform calculations on the information in a database to help you make quick, accurate and informed decisions.

Create Reports

You can use the information in a database to create professionally designed reports.

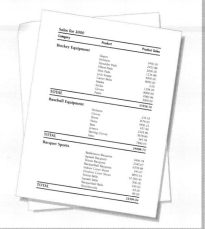

DATABASE BASICS

Table

Database programs store information in tables. A table is a collection of information about a specific topic, such as a mailing or product list. You can have one or more tables in a database. A table consists of fields and records.

Address ID	First Name	Last Name	Address	City	State/Province	Postal Code
1	Jim	Schmith	258 Linton Ave.	New York	NY	10010
2	Brenda	Petterson	50 Tree Lane	Boston	MA	02117
3	Todd	Talbot	68 Cracker Ave.	San Francisco	CA	94110
4	Chuck	Dean	47 Crosby Ave.	Las Vegas	NV	89116
5	Melanie	Robinson	26 Arnold Cres.	Jacksonville	FL	32256
6	Susan	Hughes	401 Idon Dr.	Nashville	TN	37243
7	Allen	Toppins	10 Heldon St.	Atlanta	GA	30375
8	Greg	Kilkenny	36 Buzzard St.	Boston	MA	02118
9	Jason	Marcuson	15 Bizzo Pl.	New York	NY	10020
10	Jim	Martin	890 Apple St.	San Diego	CA	92121

Record

A record is a collection of information about one person, place or thing in a table. For example, a record can contain the name and address of one client.

Field

A field is a specific category of information in a table. For example, a field can contain the first names of all your clients.

Field Name

A field name identifies the information contained in a field.

Form

Database programs provide forms you can use to quickly view, enter and change the information stored in a table. A form usually displays one record at a time and displays boxes that clearly show you where to enter information.

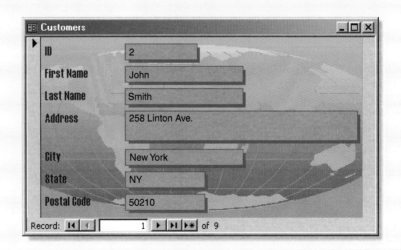

DATABASE

Sort

Database programs allow you to change the order of information in a database. For example, you can alphabetically sort all clients by last name. Sorting can help you keep track of the information in a database.

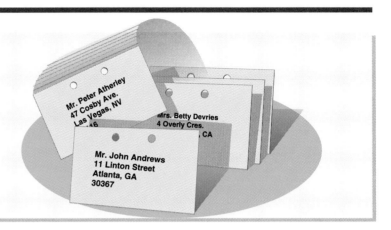

Find

You can quickly locate information of interest in a database. For example, you can search for the name of a particular client.

Query

A database program allows you to create queries to gather information of interest in a database.

When you create a query, you ask a database program to find information that meets certain criteria, or conditions. For example, you can create a query to find clients living in California who purchased more than $100 of a specific product last year.

TYPES OF DATABASES

Most database programs allow you to create two types of databases–flat file and relational.

Flat File Database

A flat file database stores information in a single table.

A flat file database is easy to set up and learn. This type of database is ideal for simple lists, such as phone number and mailing lists.

EMPLOYEE PHONE NUMBERS

Name	Department	Phone Number
Allison, Steve	Accounting	555-1762
Atherly, Peter	Sales	555-2298
Boshart, Mark	Ordering	555-1270
Coleman, Dale	Sales	555-8851
Lang, Kristin	Shipping	555-9993
Lippert, Janet	Accounting	555-0042
Oram, Derek	Maintenance	555-7148
Sanvido, Dean	Service	555-0128
Smith, John	Sales	555-7018
Talbot, Mark	Ordering	555-1510

Relational Database

A relational database stores information in two or more tables.

CLIENT ADDRESSES

Client #	Address	City	State
521	15 River St.	La Jolia	CA
522	82 15th Ave.	New York	NY
523	24 Ladner Cr.	Cleveland	OH
524	7 Pindar Rd.	Seattle	WA
525	60 Norfolk St.	Salem	NH
526	31 6th Ave.	New York	NY
527	116 West St.	Marietta	GA

ORDER INFORMATION

Client #	Product	Quantity
521	C28505	30
522	C48851	100
523	C33709	300
524	C40287	25
525	C58209	150
526	C48852	20
527	C29856	35

INVENTORY

Product	Price	In Stock
C28505	$80.00	12468
C48851	$20.00	1469
C33709	$30.00	50277
C40287	$45.00	6588
C58209	$19.99	206
C48852	$14.99	995
C29856	$79.00	50

Each table in a relational database contains information on a different topic, such as client addresses, order information or inventory.

The tables are related, or linked. If you change the information in one table, the same information will automatically change in all other tables.

A relational database is powerful and flexible, but can be more difficult to set up and learn than a flat file database. A relational database is ideal for invoicing, accounting and inventory.

IMAGE EDITOR

An image editor is a program that allows you to change the appearance of an image on your computer.

You can use a scanner or digital camera to transfer images to your computer. You can also obtain images from the Internet or purchase ready-made images, called clip-art, at most computer stores.

Popular image editors include Adobe Photoshop and Jasc Paint Shop Pro.

BITMAP IMAGES

Image editors allow you to work with bitmap images. Information about bitmap images, such as color, is stored in bits. Bit is short for binary digit and is the smallest unit of data a computer can use. When you use an image editor to change the appearance of an image, you alter the bits in the image.

FILE FORMAT

Bitmap images are available in many different file formats, including BMP, TIFF, JPEG and GIF. Many scanned images use the TIFF file format, while most images on the Web use the JPEG or GIF file format. Image editors let you open, edit and save images in several file formats.

JPEG   GIF

IMAGE EDITOR APPLICATIONS

Painting Tools

Image editors provide a variety of tools you can use to create your own images or paint and draw on existing images.

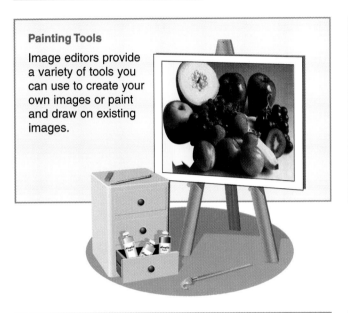

Visual Effects

Most image editors let you use visual effects to enhance an image. For example, you can change the shape of an image or add a shadow to an image. You can also combine different images to create a new image.

Optimize Web Images

Some image editors can help you optimize images for use on the Web. For example, you can use an image editor to reduce the file size of an image so that it will transfer quickly over the Internet.

Photo Enhancement

Image editors offer tools that allow you to enhance photos. For example, you can increase the brightness of a photo or remove red-eye problems.

DESKTOP PUBLISHING

A Desktop Publishing (DTP) program helps you create professional documents by integrating text and images on a page.

Popular desktop publishing programs include Adobe PageMaker and QuarkXPress.

You can use a desktop publishing program to create newsletters, brochures, flyers, advertisements, magazines and books.

TEXT

You can enter text directly into a desktop publishing document. You can also enter text into a word processor and then place the text in a desktop publishing document.

Wrap Text

A desktop publishing program lets you change the way text flows around an image.

Leading and Tracking

You can make text easier to read by changing the leading and tracking. Leading is the spacing between lines of text. Tracking is the space between characters.

Leading　　　　**Tracking**

Font

You can enhance the appearance of a document by using different character styles and sizes.

IMAGES

A desktop publishing program gives you
control over the images in a document.

Get Images

Many desktop publishing programs include a
collection of ready-made images, called clip art, that
you can use. You can also find images on the Internet
or use a digital camera or scanner to transfer images
to your computer. Make sure
you have permission to use
any images you
did not create
yourself.

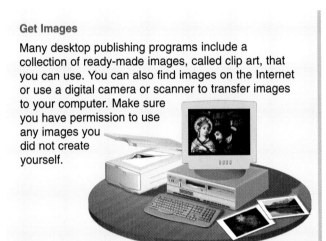

Work With Images

You can move, size and rotate images in a desktop
publishing document.

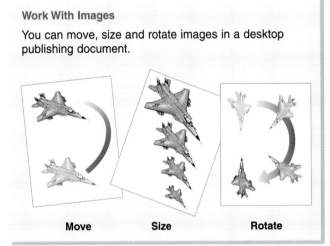

| Move | Size | Rotate |

PAGE LAYOUT

A desktop publishing program includes features
that help you design pages in a document.

Master Page

A master page contains formatting that is repeated
throughout a document, such as page numbers
and headings.

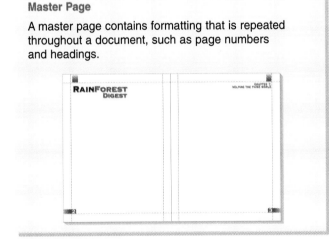

Paragraph Style

A paragraph style is a group of settings you save
and then apply to sections of text in a document.
Paragraph styles save you time and help give the
document a consistent design.

APPLICATION SUITE

An application suite is a collection of programs sold together in one package.

Microsoft Office is the most popular application suite. Other application suites include Corel WordPerfect Office and Lotus SmartSuite.

ADVANTAGES

Cost

Buying programs as part of an application suite costs less than buying each program individually.

Easy to Use

Programs in an application suite share a common design and work in a similar way. Once you learn one program, you can easily learn the others.

DISADVANTAGE

Since all the programs in an application suite come from the same manufacturer, you may not get the best combination of features for your needs. Make sure you evaluate all the programs in an application suite before making your purchase.

APPLICATION SUITE PROGRAMS

Application suites commonly include the following types of programs. Some application suites also offer additional programs, such as a desktop publishing program that helps you design professional documents.

Word Processing Program

A word processing program lets you create documents, such as letters and reports.

Spreadsheet Program

A spreadsheet program lets you manage and analyze financial information.

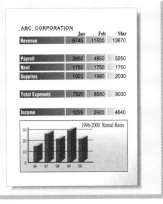

Presentation Program

A presentation program lets you design professional presentations.

Information Management Program

An information management program can help you manage your e-mail messages, appointments, contacts, memos and tasks.

Database Program

A database program lets you manage large collections of information. A database program may only be included in higher-priced versions of an application suite.

UTILITY SOFTWARE

A utility is a program that performs a specific task on your computer.

You can buy many utility programs at computer stores. Some utility programs are also available free of charge on the Internet.

The utilities you can use depend on the operating system running on your computer.

Norton Utilities

Symantec's Norton Utilities provides tools to help you maintain and optimize your computer. Norton Utilities also includes tools to help you recover lost files and protect against computer failure.

VirusScan

McAfee's VirusScan is an anti-virus program you can use to reduce the risk of a virus infecting your computer. A virus is a program that can cause problems such as affecting the performance of your computer and erasing the information on your hard drive.

Acrobat Reader

Adobe Acrobat Reader is a program that allows you to view Portable Document Format (PDF) files. These files are often used on the World Wide Web to display books and magazines exactly as they appear in printed form.

ViaVoice

IBM's ViaVoice is a speech recognition program that allows you to control your computer with your voice. You can speak to your computer to perform tasks such as opening files, searching the World Wide Web or dictating documents you want to create.

WinFax Pro

With Symantec WinFax Pro, you can use your computer's fax modem to send and receive faxes. WinFax Pro allows you to convert the faxes you receive into documents you can edit using a word processor.

WinZip

WinZip Computing's WinZip helps you decompress files. Many of the files on the Internet are compressed, or squeezed together, and must be decompressed before you can use them on your computer.

WinZip also compresses information so files can transfer faster between computers.

GAME SOFTWARE

Game software lets you play games on your computer.

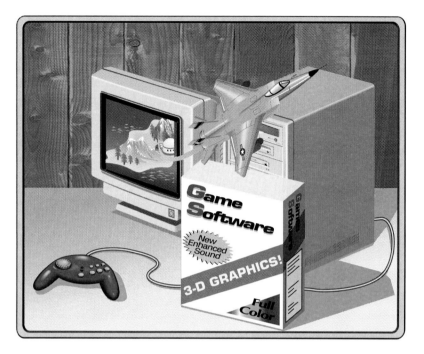

There are many different types of games available, including action, sports, strategy, simulation, puzzle and educational games. Games are available for all ages and skill levels.

GAME CONSIDERATIONS

Purchase Games

You can buy games at computer stores. There are also many games available on the Internet. Games can be expensive, but game manufacturers often offer a trial version, or demo version, of their games for free on the Internet. This allows you to try a game before you buy it.

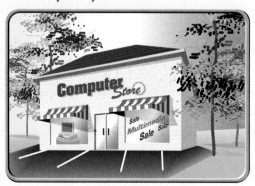

Internet and Network Games

Many games are designed to let multiple people compete against each other on the Internet or on a network.

There are many online gaming services available that allow you to easily connect to other people on the Internet to play a game. When you play a game with other people on the Internet, each person usually has to have their own copy of the game.

GAME HARDWARE

Game Controller

A game controller is a device, such as a joystick or gamepad, that allows you to interact with a game. Popular game controllers include the Microsoft SideWinder joystick and Gravis GamePad.

Some game controllers offer enhanced features. For example, you can obtain a game controller that will move in response to actions in a game or one that offers extra controls.

Some games require a specific type of game controller. Before buying a game, check to see what type of controller the game requires.

3D Graphics Accelerator Card

Many games are designed with 3D graphics and run best on a computer with a 3D graphics accelerator card.

A 3D graphics accelerator card is a circuit board that translates complex instructions from the computer into a form the monitor can understand. Popular 3D graphics accelerator cards include Matrox Millennium, ATI Radeon and 3dfx Voodoo.

Some games require a specific type of 3D graphics card. Before buying a game, check to see what type of card the game requires.

CHAPTER 6

Operating Systems

What is an operating system and which one is best for you? This chapter provides the information you are looking for.

INTRODUCTION TO OPERATING SYSTEMS

An operating system is the software that controls the overall activity of a computer.

An operating system ensures that all parts of a computer system work together smoothly and efficiently.

OPERATING SYSTEM FUNCTIONS

Control Hardware

An operating system controls the different parts of a computer system and enables all the parts to work together.

Run Software

An operating system runs software, such as Microsoft Word and Corel Quattro Pro.

Manage Information

An operating system provides ways to manage and organize information stored on a computer. You can use an operating system to sort, copy, move, delete or view files.

TYPES OF OPERATING SYSTEMS

MS-DOS

MS-DOS stands for Microsoft Disk Operating System. MS-DOS displays lines of text on the screen. You perform tasks by typing text commands.

Windows

Windows is a Graphical User Interface (GUI, pronounced "gooey"). A GUI allows you to use pictures instead of text commands to perform tasks. This makes Windows easier to use than MS-DOS.

UNIX

UNIX is a powerful operating system used by many computers on the Internet. There are many different versions of the UNIX operating system available.

Mac OS

Mac OS is a Graphical User Interface (GUI) for Macintosh computers.

PLATFORM

A platform refers to the type of operating system used by a computer, such as Windows or UNIX. Programs used on one platform will not usually work on another platform. For example, you cannot use Word for Windows on a computer running UNIX.

MS-DOS

MS-DOS is an operating system that performs tasks using text commands you enter.

MS-DOS stands for Microsoft Disk Operating System.

Command Prompt

The command prompt (C:\>) tells you that MS-DOS is ready to accept a command.

Cursor

The cursor is the flashing line on the screen. The cursor indicates where the text you type will appear.

Command

You enter a command to perform a task or start a program. A single command can usually tell the computer what you want to accomplish. For example, the DATE command tells the computer to display the current date.

FILE ORGANIZATION

Like folders in a filing cabinet, MS-DOS uses directories to organize the data stored on a computer.

The root directory (C:\) is the main directory. All other directories are located within this directory.

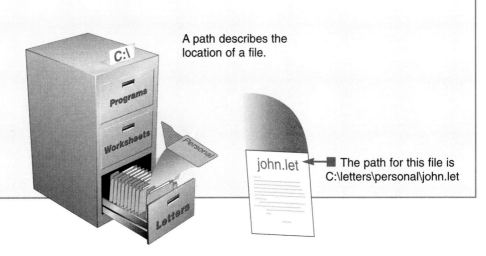

A path describes the location of a file.

john.let ◄ The path for this file is C:\letters\personal\john.let

FILE NAME

When you store a file on a computer, you must give the file a name. An MS-DOS file name cannot contain any spaces. A file name consists of a name and an extension, separated by a period.

The **name** describes the contents of a file and can have up to eight characters.

The **extension** identifies the type of file and consists of three characters.

UTILITIES

Some versions of MS-DOS include special programs, called utilities, to protect files and optimize a computer. For example, the ScanDisk program finds and repairs disk errors.

Windows 3.1 works with MS-DOS to control the overall activity of a computer. Windows 3.1 is not a true operating system since it needs MS-DOS to operate.

Windows 3.1 displays pictures on the screen to help you perform tasks.

Program Manager

The Program Manager is the control center where you start programs.

Program Icon

A program icon lets you start a program, such as a word processor. An icon is a small picture that represents an item, such as a program.

Window

A window is a rectangle that displays information on the screen. Each window has a title bar that displays the name of the window (example: Accessories).

Group Icon

A group icon contains program icons. For example, the Games group icon contains several games.

File Manager

The File Manager lets you view and organize all the files stored on your computer. Windows 3.1 uses directories to organize information, just as you would use folders to organize papers in a filing cabinet.

Desktop

The desktop is the background area of the screen.

Windows 95 is the successor to Windows 3.1. This operating system is more graphical and easier to use than Windows 3.1.

Windows 95 is a true operating system because it does not need MS-DOS to operate.

My Computer

My Computer lets you browse through all the folders and documents stored on your computer.

Recycle Bin

The Recycle Bin stores the documents you delete and allows you to recover them later.

Network Neighborhood

Network Neighborhood lets you view the folders and files available on your network.

Start Button

The Start button lets you quickly access programs and documents.

Taskbar

The taskbar contains the Start button and displays the name of each open window on the screen.

Windows Explorer

Windows Explorer shows you the location of each folder and document on your computer. You can use Windows Explorer to move, open, print or delete documents.

Shortcut

A shortcut provides a quick way to open a document or program you use regularly.

Windows 98 is the successor to Windows 95. This operating system is very similar to Windows 95 but includes many new and improved features.

There are currently two versions of Windows 98. Windows 98 Second Edition includes many enhancements and updates to the original version of Windows 98.

You can check your Windows 98 CD-ROM disc to determine whether you have Windows 98 Second Edition installed on your computer.

My Documents

My Documents provides a convenient place to store your documents.

Internet Explorer

Internet Explorer lets you browse through information on the World Wide Web.

Quick Launch Toolbar

The Quick Launch Toolbar lets you quickly access commonly used features, including Internet Explorer and Outlook Express.

WINDOWS 98 FEATURES

Computer Maintenance

Windows 98 is more reliable than Windows 95 and includes many tools you can use to find and fix problems with your computer. For example, you can check your hard drive for errors, remove unnecessary files and defragment your hard drive to improve its performance.

FAT32

FAT32 is a file system that better manages data on large hard drives to reduce wasted space. Windows 98 can convert your hard drive to FAT32 without disrupting your current programs and documents.

Multiple Monitor Capability

Windows 98 has the ability to display the Windows desktop on multiple monitors. This makes working with several open documents or programs easier.

Internet

Windows 98 includes several programs that allow you to view and exchange information on the Internet, including Internet Explorer, Outlook Express and FrontPage Express. Outlook Express lets you exchange electronic mail with people around the world. FrontPage Express allows you to create your own Web pages.

WINDOWS ME

Windows Me is the successor to Windows 98. Windows Me stands for Windows Millennium Edition.

If you have used Windows 98, you will already be familiar with the way Windows Me looks and works.

WINDOWS ME FEATURES

Record Videos

Windows Me allows you to record, edit and save videos on your computer using Windows Movie Maker. Once you have finished working with a video, you can e-mail the video to your friends and colleagues or place the video on a Web page.

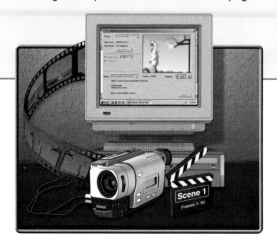

Manage Multimedia Files

Windows Me contains an enhanced version of Windows Media Player that helps you manage your multimedia files. You can use Windows Media Player to play a variety of multimedia files and listen to radio stations over the Internet.

Restore Your Computer

If you are experiencing problems with your computer, you can use the System Restore feature to return your computer to a time before the problems occurred. For example, if you have accidentally deleted program files, you can restore your computer to a time before you deleted the files.

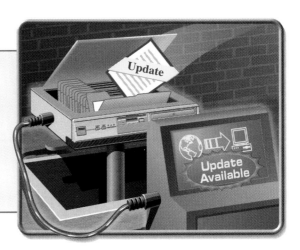

Set Up a Home Network

If you have more than one computer at home, you can use the Home Networking Wizard to help you set up a network so you can exchange information between the computers. A home network is also useful for sharing equipment and playing multiplayer games.

Update Windows

The Windows Update feature allows you to automatically update your computer with the latest Windows features available on the Internet. When you are connected to the Internet, Windows will automatically check for updates, determine which updates apply to your computer and notify you when the updates are available.

WINDOWS NT

Windows NT is a powerful version of the Windows operating system that provides advanced networking and security features.

Windows NT is available in two main versions.

Windows NT Workstation

Windows NT Workstation is a version of the Windows NT operating system that is used on client/server and some peer-to-peer networks.

Many powerful applications are designed specifically to run on Windows NT Workstation. Many programs designed for the Windows 95 and Windows 98 operating systems will also perform better on Windows NT Workstation.

Windows NT Server

Windows NT Server is a version of the Windows NT operating system that is used on client/server networks. Windows NT Server is designed to support the heavy processing demands of a network server.

The client computers on a network running Windows NT Server can use a variety of operating systems, such as Linux, Windows 98 and Mac OS 9.

Windows 2000 is the successor to Windows NT. This operating system offers improved networking and security features.

There are several versions of Windows 2000 available.

Windows 2000 Professional

Windows 2000 Professional is commonly used on client/server networks but can also be used on peer-to-peer networks. This operating system offers increased stability and provides tools that can help you maintain your computer. Windows 2000 Professional is intended for business use.

Windows 2000 Server and Windows 2000 Advanced Server

Windows 2000 Server and Windows 2000 Advanced Server are found on large client/server networks. These operating systems are both designed to support heavy network processing demands. Windows 2000 Advanced Server can support a larger network than Windows 2000 Server, which makes the Advanced Server version suitable for large businesses and Internet service providers.

UNIX

UNIX is an older, powerful operating system that can be used to run a single computer or an entire network.

UNIX is the oldest computer operating system still in widespread use today.

VERSIONS

Many companies have owned UNIX since its development in the late 1960s. Today, there are several versions of the UNIX operating system available.

Popular UNIX operating systems for personal computers include UnixWare by SCO, Solaris by Sun Microsystems and Linux, which is available for free on the World Wide Web. Other versions of UNIX that are more popular as network operating systems include HP-UX by Hewlett-Packard and AIX by IBM.

INTERNET

Many of the first computers used to establish the Internet ran the UNIX operating system. Even today, UNIX is the most widely used operating system for servers on the Internet.

UNIX FEATURES

Power

The UNIX operating system is very powerful. UNIX is harder to install and set up than most other operating systems, but provides greater control over a computer's resources and power.

A computer's performance may be significantly improved when running UNIX.

Multitasking

UNIX was originally developed as the operating system for a single large computer, called a mainframe computer. Since multiple users can access a mainframe computer at the same time, UNIX was developed to run many programs and perform numerous tasks at once, called multitasking.

UNIX's multitasking capabilities make it an efficient operating system for networks.

Security

UNIX has many built-in security features to protect information from being accidentally deleted or accessed by unauthorized users.

UNIX's strong security features are one of the reasons UNIX is such a popular operating system on the Internet.

Linux is a UNIX-based operating system that is available for free on the World Wide Web.

Many companies, such as Red Hat and Mandrake, create easy-to-use versions of Linux that you can purchase.

Red Hat Linux is a popular version of Linux that comes with the GNOME desktop environment. GNOME displays pictures on the screen to help you perform tasks.

Home directory

The Home directory allows you to browse through the folder that stores your personal files.

Help Web Pages

The Help Web pages let you quickly display Web pages that offer help on using Linux.

GNOME Panel

The GNOME Panel contains the Main Menu button and Application Launchers and displays the name of each open window on the screen.

Main Menu Button

The Main Menu button gives you quick access to programs.

Application Launchers

Application Launchers allow you to quickly access commonly used programs, such as the help system and Netscape Communicator.

LINUX FEATURES

Software

Red Hat Linux includes a wide variety of software, such as a drawing program, spreadsheet program, calendar program and a simple text editor. You will also find an on-screen calculator, an address book and many games that you can play.

Accounts

When you install Linux, the root account and one or more user accounts are created. You can work in Linux using either the root account or a personal account. The root account is useful for performing administrative and maintenance tasks. When performing daily tasks, you should work in a user account. You can set up a different user account for each person who uses your computer.

Command Line

You can work in Linux using a Graphical User Interface (GUI) such as GNOME or using the command line. The command line displays text without any graphics. Working in the command line allows you to perform many tasks more quickly than in a GUI, though you must know the proper commands.

MAC OS 9

Mac OS 9 is a popular
version of the Macintosh
operating system.

MAC OS 9 FEATURES

Multimedia

Mac OS 9 includes the QuickTime
player program, which allows you to
manage and play multimedia files
such as music and movie clips.

Voice Recognition

Mac OS 9 offers a speech recognition
program that allows your computer to
recognize voice commands. You can also
use the Voiceprint Password feature to
use your voice as a password when you
start your computer.

Internet

Mac OS 9 offers several features that help
you find and exchange information on the
Internet. For example, the Sherlock 2
feature allows you to efficiently search for
information in categories such as News,
Reference, People and Shopping.

MAC OS X

Mac OS X (ten) is the latest version of the Macintosh operating system.

MAC OS X FEATURES

Graphical User Interface

Mac OS X offers a new Graphical User Interface (GUI) that is designed to make the operating system easier to use than previous versions. The new GUI features photo-quality icons and an area at the bottom of the screen, called the Dock, where you can store items you frequently access.

Graphics

Mac OS X combines several advanced graphics technologies, including Portable Document Format (PDF), QuickTime and OpenGL, to provide enhanced graphics capabilities. This improves the display of graphics in programs such as desktop publishing programs and games.

Operating System Core

Mac OS X offers an improved operating system core, or kernel. This improved kernel helps ensure that your computer hardware and software work together efficiently and provides more stability than previous versions of the Macintosh operating system.

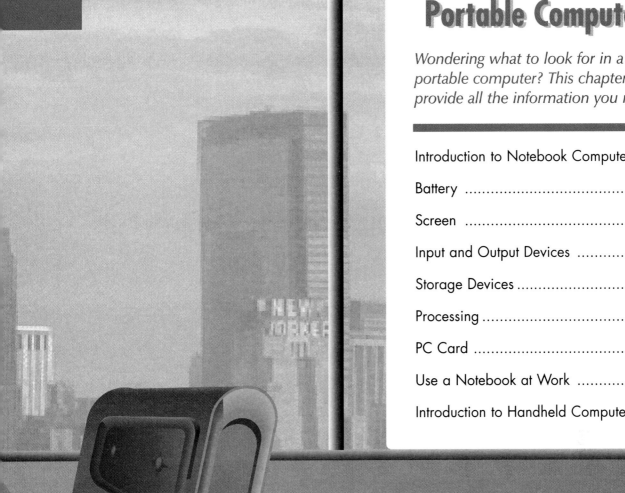

CHAPTER 7

Portable Computers

Wondering what to look for in a portable computer? This chapter will provide all the information you need.

INTRODUCTION TO NOTEBOOK COMPUTERS

A notebook is a small, lightweight computer that you can easily transport.

A notebook computer is also called a laptop.

You can buy a notebook computer with the same capabilities as a full-size computer, although notebook computers are more expensive.

A notebook computer has a built-in keyboard, pointing device and screen. This eliminates the need for cables to connect these devices to the notebook.

ADVANTAGES OF NOTEBOOKS

Travel

A notebook computer lets you work when traveling or outdoors. You can also use a notebook computer to bring work home instead of staying late at the office.

Presentations

You can bring a notebook computer to meetings to present information.

BATTERY

A battery or an electrical outlet can supply the power for a notebook computer.

A battery lets you use a notebook when no electrical outlets are available.

TYPES OF BATTERIES

There are two main types of batteries–Nickel Metal Hydride (NiMH) and lithium-ion. Lithium-ion is a more expensive battery, but is lighter and lasts longer than NiMH. Some notebook computers now use Smart batteries. Smart batteries help notebooks better manage power consumption.

MONITOR A BATTERY

Most notebooks display the amount of battery power remaining, either on the screen or on a panel built into the computer.

RECHARGE A BATTERY

The power supplied by most batteries lasts for only a few hours. You must recharge a battery before you can use it again. If you are unable to recharge a battery when traveling, bring an extra battery so you can work for a longer period of time.

SCREEN

The screen on a notebook computer uses Liquid Crystal Display (LCD). This is the same type of display found in most digital wristwatches.

An LCD screen uses very little power, which extends the length of time you can use a battery before needing to recharge. An LCD screen also weighs much less than a full-size monitor, which makes a notebook easier to carry.

BACKLIGHT

Notebooks have an internal light source that illuminates the back of the screen. This makes the screen easier to view in poorly lit areas but shortens the length of time you can use a battery before needing to recharge.

USE A FULL-SIZE MONITOR

Most notebooks can use both the notebook screen and a full-size monitor at the same time. This feature is very useful when delivering presentations.

SCREEN SIZE

The size of the screen is measured diagonally. Screen sizes range from about 12 to 15 inches.

TYPES OF SCREENS

Passive Matrix

This type of screen is less expensive than an active matrix screen, but is not as bright or rich in color. The lower cost makes a passive matrix screen ideal for routine office tasks.

A dual-scan screen is an enhanced version of a passive matrix screen that offers improved clarity.

Passive matrix screens can be difficult to read when viewed from an angle. This is ideal when you want to keep work private from people sitting next to you on a train or plane, but makes delivering a presentation to several people difficult.

Active Matrix

This type of screen is more expensive, but displays brighter, richer colors than a passive matrix screen.

An active matrix screen is also called a Thin-Film Transistor (TFT) screen.

You can view an active matrix screen from wide angles, which makes it more suitable for delivering presentations to several people.

INPUT AND OUTPUT DEVICES

POINTING DEVICES

There are several devices that let you move the pointer around the screen of a notebook computer.

A mouse is impractical when traveling, since you need a relatively large, flat surface to move the mouse.

Pointing Stick

A pointing stick is a small device that resembles an eraser. You push a pointing stick in different directions to move the pointer on the screen.

Trackball

A trackball is an upside-down mouse that remains stationary. You roll the ball with your fingers or palm to move the pointer on the screen.

Touchpad

A touchpad is a surface that is sensitive to pressure and motion. When you move your fingertip across the pad, the pointer on the screen moves in the same direction.

KEYBOARD

The keys on a notebook keyboard may be small and close together to save space. Before buying a notebook, type several paragraphs of text to make sure the keyboard is suitable for you.

Some notebook computers have a keyboard that expands to a full-size keyboard.

MODEM

You can buy a notebook with a built-in modem or add modem capabilities later.

A modem allows you to connect to the Internet to exchange information and messages.

When traveling, a modem also lets you connect to the network at work.

SOUND CARD AND SPEAKERS

You can buy a notebook with a built-in sound card and speakers to play and record sound. This is very useful when you want to use the notebook to deliver presentations.

STORAGE DEVICES

HARD DRIVE

The hard drive is the primary device a notebook uses to store information. Buy the largest hard drive you can afford. New programs and data will quickly fill a hard drive.

FLOPPY DRIVE

Many notebooks come with a floppy drive that allows you to store and retrieve information on floppy disks.

If you will not use a floppy drive very often, you can buy a notebook without a floppy drive to reduce the notebook's weight. You can then connect the notebook to an external floppy drive when necessary.

CD-ROM OR DVD-ROM DRIVE

A notebook computer can include a CD-ROM drive or a DVD-ROM drive to read information stored on Compact Discs (CDs) or Digital Versatile Discs (DVDs).

Some notebooks let you remove the CD-ROM or DVD-ROM drive and replace it with another component. This new component could be an extra battery to increase the amount of time you can use the notebook, a second hard drive for additional storage space or a floppy drive.

CPU

The Central Processing Unit (CPU) is the main chip in a computer. The CPU processes instructions, performs calculations and manages the flow of information through a computer system.

Special CPUs, called mobile CPUs, are developed for notebook computers. Mobile CPUs are smaller and consume less power than traditional CPUs.

This chart shows common CPUs available for notebook computers. The CPU you decide to buy will depend on your budget and how you plan to use the computer.

CPU	SPEED (MHz)
Intel Celeron	400 450 500 550 600 650 700
Intel Pentium II	266 300 333 366 400
Intel Pentium III	600 650 700 750 800 850
AMD-K6-III	450 475 500
AMD-K6-2	500 533 550
Transmeta Crusoe	500 600 700

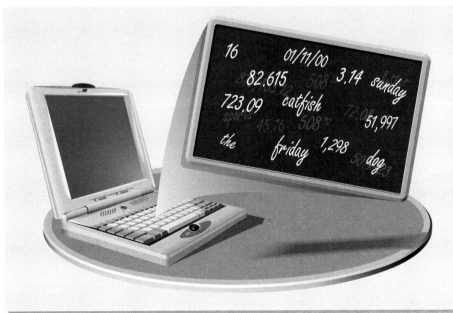

MEMORY

Electronic memory, or RAM, temporarily stores data inside a computer. Memory works like a blackboard that is constantly overwritten with new data. A notebook computer running Windows Me should have at least 32 MB of memory to ensure that programs run smoothly.

PC CARD

A PC Card adds a new capability, such as additional memory, to a notebook computer.

Some PC Cards provide multiple features. For example, a single PC Card can provide networking and modem capabilities.

A PC Card used to be called a PCMCIA Card. PCMCIA stands for Personal Computer Memory Card International Association.

TYPES OF PC CARDS

A PC Card is a lightweight device about the size of a credit card. There are three types of PC Cards–Type I, Type II and Type III. Type I is the thinnest card, while Type III is the thickest. Each type of card can vary in the features it offers.

PC SLOT

You insert a PC Card into a slot on a notebook computer. Most notebook computers have a PC slot that can accept both a Type I and Type II PC Card or one Type III PC Card.

NETWORK INTERFACE CARD

A network interface card connects a notebook to a network and controls the flow of information between the network and the notebook. When connected to a network, you can access all the equipment and information available on the network.

INFRARED PORT

Some notebook computers have an infrared port to share information without using cables. Infrared ports are commonly used for connecting a notebook computer to a printer.

PORT REPLICATOR

A port replicator lets you connect many devices, such as a printer, modem and mouse, to a notebook at once. After you connect a port replicator to a notebook, you can use all the devices attached to the port replicator without having to attach each device to the notebook individually.

DOCKING STATION

A docking station lets you connect many devices to a notebook at once. A docking station can also provide additional features, such as networking capabilities and a full-size monitor and keyboard.

INTRODUCTION TO HANDHELD COMPUTERS

A handheld computer is a portable computer that is small enough to carry in your hand.

PDAs

A Personal Digital Assistant (PDA) is a popular type of handheld computer that commonly offers electronic organizer capabilities. PDAs have an electronic pen, called a stylus, that you can use to input information. You can also purchase a collapsible keyboard for some types of PDAs. Popular PDAs include Palm Inc.'s Palm computers and Casio's Pocket PCs.

OTHER HANDHELD COMPUTERS

Some handheld computers, such as Hewlett-Packard's Jornada, are more like small desktop computers than electronic organizers. These types of handheld computers usually have a built-in keyboard. In comparison to a PDA, these handheld computers have more storage capacity and typically come with larger screens.

HANDHELD COMPUTER APPLICATIONS

Electronic Organizers

Handheld computers are capable of storing thousands of addresses, appointments and memos. Most handheld computers also come with scheduling software, such as a calendar program.

Exchange Information

You can connect a handheld computer to a desktop computer to exchange data between the two computers. For example, you may want to transfer information, such as appointments, from your handheld computer to your desktop computer.

Internet Access

You can use some handheld computers to connect to the Internet. You can purchase a handheld computer with built-in Internet capabilities or add Internet capabilities later.

OPERATING SYSTEMS

Most handheld computers use either the Palm OS or Windows CE operating system to control the overall activity of the computer.

Palm OS and Windows CE are Graphical User Interfaces (GUI, pronounced "gooey"). A GUI allows you to use pictures instead of text commands to perform tasks.

CHAPTER 8

Macintosh Computers

Wondering what a Mac is? This chapter will introduce you to Macintosh computers.

INTRODUCTION TO MACINTOSH COMPUTERS

Macintosh computers, or Macs, were introduced by Apple Computer in 1984. Macintosh computers were the first home computers with a mouse, on-screen windows, menus and icons.

MACINTOSH FEATURES

Easy to Set Up and Use

Macintosh computers are easy to set up, which allows you to quickly get started using a new Macintosh computer. The graphical interface of a Macintosh makes this type of computer easy to work with.

Desktop Publishing

The fast display of images on screen and true What You See Is What You Get (WYSIWYG) display have helped to establish Macintosh computers as the standard in the desktop publishing industry. Desktop publishing lets you create professional documents by integrating text and graphics on a page.

OPERATING SYSTEMS

Like the Windows operating systems, Macintosh operating systems use a Graphical User Interface (GUI, pronounced "gooey"). A GUI allows you to use pictures instead of text commands to perform tasks.

Many Macintosh computers use the Mac OS 9 operating system, which offers advanced Internet features. The Mac OS 9 operating system improves on previous versions of the Macintosh operating system, such as Mac OS 8.

The latest version of the Macintosh operating system is Mac OS X. This version offers many new features, including a new graphical user interface.

CPUs

The Central Processing Unit (CPU), also called a processor, is the main chip in a computer. A CPU processes instructions, performs calculations and manages the flow of information through a computer system.

300-500 MHz

400-500 MHz

Macintosh computers currently use Motorola's PowerPC G3 or PowerPC G4 processor. The PowerPC G3 processor is available with speeds ranging from 300 MHz to 500 MHz. The PowerPC G4 processor is available with speeds ranging from 400 MHz to 500 MHz.

POWER MAC G4

Apple Computer's Power Mac G4 is currently the most powerful type of Macintosh computer.

The Power Mac G4 uses a PowerPC G4 processor.

DUAL PROCESSOR

Some Power Mac G4 computers use two G4 processors to provide increased processing speed and power. This is useful for business users who work with programs that require high processing capabilities, such as desktop publishing programs.

UPGRADE

You can easily expand the capabilities of a Power Mac G4 computer as your needs increase. The Power Mac G4 is designed with room for you to add additional features. For example, a Power Mac G4 can accommodate up to three hard drives.

MULTIMEDIA

The Power Mac G4 provides advanced multimedia capabilities. For example, the Power Mac G4 comes with video editing software and can easily accommodate high-speed devices, such as a digital video camera.

The Power Mac G4 Cube is a Macintosh computer that is less than a quarter of the size of most tower computers.

The Power Mac G4 Cube is only 8 inches high and 8 inches wide and features an innovative computer case design.

QUIET

The Power Mac G4 Cube uses a convection system to cool the inside of the computer instead of using a fan. This allows the Power Mac G4 Cube to operate more quietly than other computers.

EASY TO UPGRADE

The Power Mac G4 Cube is designed so that you can slide the internal components from the computer case for easy access. This makes the Power Mac G4 Cube easy to upgrade. For example, you can easily add more memory to the Power Mac G4 Cube.

iMAC

The iMac is an inexpensive, Internet-ready Macintosh computer that is designed to meet the needs of most home computer users.

ALL-IN-ONE COMPUTER

The iMac is an all-in-one computer that contains components such as a monitor, speakers, hard drive and CD-ROM or DVD-ROM drive in a single unit. This makes the iMac easy for new computer users to set up and use.

PORTABLE

The iMac's all-in-one design makes it easy to move the iMac to a new location without having to set the computer up again. There is also a handle at the back of the iMac that you can use to help you move the computer.

UNIQUE DESIGN

The iMac has a unique design and is available in a variety of colors. For example, you can buy an iMac in colors such as Ruby and Sage.

SOFTWARE

The iMac comes with software that home users will find useful. For example, you can use the iMovie program to create and edit home movies and the Quicken program to manage your personal finances.

NO INTERNAL FLOPPY DRIVE

The iMac was the first full-size computer to come without a floppy drive. If you want to store information on floppy disks, you can purchase an external floppy drive that you can easily connect to your iMac.

INTERNET ACCESS

The iMac comes with a built-in modem and software you can use to access the Internet. This can help you quickly get started browsing the World Wide Web and exchanging e-mail with other people on the Internet.

The iBook and PowerBook are Macintosh notebook computers. Like other notebook computers, the iBook and PowerBook are small, lightweight and easy to transport.

iBook and PowerBook computers use a PowerPC G3 processor.

iBOOK

The iBook is an inexpensive notebook computer that is designed to meet the needs of most home computer users. The iBook has a unique design that is similar to the iMac computer and is available in a variety of colors.

POWERBOOK

The PowerBook is a powerful notebook computer that is useful for business use. For example, the PowerBook is useful for creating multimedia presentations or performing complex spreadsheet calculations. You can buy a PowerBook with the same capabilities as a full-size computer.

A port is a connector at the back of a computer where you plug in an external device. Most Macintosh computers come with the following ports.

FireWire

A FireWire port allows you to attach up to 63 devices to your computer using a single port. FireWire connections are faster than other types of connections, which makes them ideal for connecting multimedia and high-speed devices such as video cameras, digital cameras and external hard drives. Most new Macintosh computers come with one or two FireWire ports.

Network Port

A network port connects the computer to a network.

USB Port

A USB port allows you to connect up to 127 devices using a single port. For example, you can use a USB port to connect a printer, modem and joystick to your computer. Most Macintosh computers come with one or two Universal Serial Bus (USB) ports.

Speaker Port

A speaker port connects speakers.

Microphone Port

A microphone port connects a microphone.

Monitor Port

A monitor port connects a monitor.

INPUT AND OUTPUT DEVICES

MOUSE

A mouse is a handheld pointing device that lets you select and move items on your screen. Unlike a PC mouse, which has two buttons, a Macintosh mouse has only one button.

KEYBOARD

The keys on a keyboard let you enter information and instructions into a computer. The Macintosh keyboard has a **Command**, or **Apple**, key (⌘ ⌘) that you can use to quickly perform specific tasks. For example, in a word processing document, you can quickly make text bold by pressing the ⌘ ⌘ and **B** keys.

MONITOR

A monitor displays text and images generated by a computer. Some monitors are designed to work only with Macintosh computers. For more flexibility, you can buy a monitor that will work with both Macs and PCs.

VIDEO CAPABILITIES

All Macintosh computers come with built-in video capabilities that translate instructions from the computer into a form the monitor can understand.

SOUND CAPABILITIES

All Macintosh computers come with built-in sound capabilities. This allows Macintosh computers to play and record sound.

MODEM

A modem lets computers exchange information through telephone lines. Most Macintosh computers have built-in modems.

PRINTER

A printer produces a paper copy of the information displayed on the screen. When buying a printer for a Macintosh computer, make sure the printer is Macintosh-compatible. A printer designed for a PC may not work with a Mac.

IMAGING DEVICE

You can purchase an imaging device for your Macintosh computer, such as a scanner, video camera or digital camera. A scanner is a device that reads images and text into a computer. A video camera or digital camera lets you store videos or pictures on your computer.

Scanner   Video Camera   Digital Camera

CHAPTER 9

Networks

How can multiple computers share information more efficiently? Learn about networks in this chapter.

INTRODUCTION TO NETWORKS

A network is a group of connected computers that allows people to share information and equipment.

LOCAL AREA NETWORK

A Local Area Network (LAN) is a network that connects computers within a small geographic area, such as a building.

Home Network

A home network is a small local area network that connects computers in a home. Home networks are often used to play multi-player games. There are home networking kits available that contain all the necessary hardware and software for creating a home network.

WIDE AREA NETWORK

A Wide Area Network (WAN) is a network that connects computers across a large geographic area, such as a city or country. A WAN can transmit information by telephone line, microwave or satellite.

NETWORK ADVANTAGES

Work Away From Office

When traveling or at home, you can connect to the network at work to exchange messages and files.

Share Information

Networks let you easily share information without having to store the information on a disk and physically carry the information from one computer to another. You can exchange information such as programs, documents, electronic mail, video, sound and images on a network.

Share Equipment

Computers connected to a network can share equipment, such as a printer or modem.

NETWORK ADMINISTRATOR

A network administrator manages the network and makes sure the network runs smoothly. A network administrator may also be called a network manager, information systems manager or system administrator.

Network Administrator

NETWORK APPLICATIONS

Electronic Mail

You can exchange electronic mail (e-mail) messages with other people on a network. Electronic mail saves paper and provides a fast, convenient way to exchange ideas and request information.

Groupware

Groupware is software that helps people on a network coordinate and manage projects. Groupware packages usually let you exchange electronic mail, schedule meetings, participate in online discussions and share corporate information. Popular groupware packages include Lotus Domino and Novell GroupWise.

Videoconferencing

Videoconferencing allows you to have face-to-face conversations with other people on a network, whether they are in the same building or on the other side of the country.

A computer must have a sound card, speakers and a microphone to transmit and receive sound. The computer must also have a video camera to transmit video images.

PARTS OF A NETWORK

Computers

A network links computers together, allowing the people using the computers to work more efficiently. A network can connect different types of computers, such as IBM-compatible and Macintosh computers.

Hub

A hub is a device that provides a central location where all the cables on a network come together.

Network Interface Card

A network interface card is an expansion card that physically connects each computer to a network. This card controls the flow of information between the network and the computer.

Cables

Cables are the wires that connect computers and equipment on a network. There are four main types of cables–coaxial, Unshielded Twisted Pair (UTP), Shielded Twisted Pair (STP) and fiber-optic.

Fiber-optic cable is the most expensive type of cable, but it can carry information faster and over longer distances than other types of cables.

PEER-TO-PEER NETWORK

The people on a peer-to-peer network store their files on their own computers. Anyone on the network can access shared files stored on another computer.

A peer-to-peer network provides a simple and inexpensive way to connect fewer than ten computers.

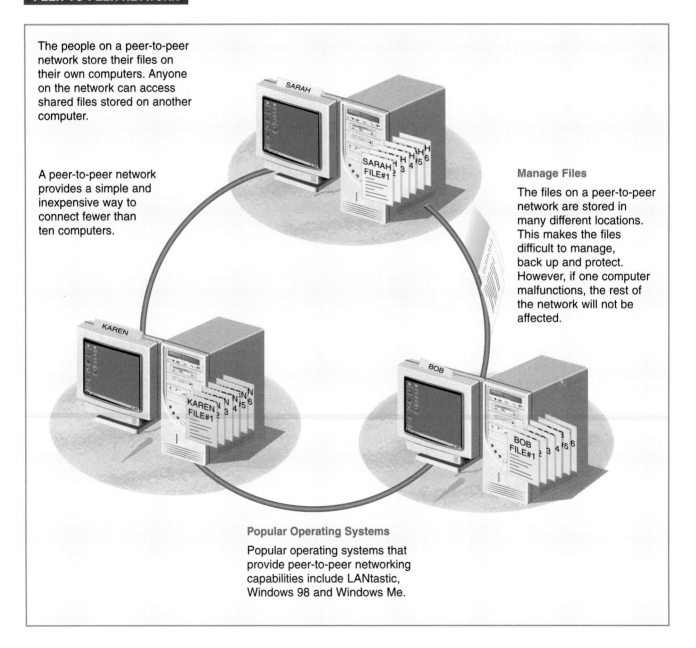

Manage Files

The files on a peer-to-peer network are stored in many different locations. This makes the files difficult to manage, back up and protect. However, if one computer malfunctions, the rest of the network will not be affected.

Popular Operating Systems

Popular operating systems that provide peer-to-peer networking capabilities include LANtastic, Windows 98 and Windows Me.

CLIENT/SERVER NETWORK

The people on a client/server network store their files on a central computer. Everyone connected to the network can access files stored on the central computer.

A client/server network provides a highly efficient way to connect ten or more computers, or computers that exchange large amounts of information.

Server

The server is the central computer that stores the files of every person on the network.

Manage Files

All the files on a client/server network are stored on the server. This makes the files easy to manage, back up and protect. However, if the server malfunctions, the entire network will be affected.

Popular Operating Systems

Popular operating systems that provide client/server networking capabilities include NetWare and Windows 2000.

Client

A client is a computer that can access information stored on the server.

ETHERNET

Ethernet is the most popular and least expensive way information can travel through a network. Ethernet is the easiest type of network to set up.

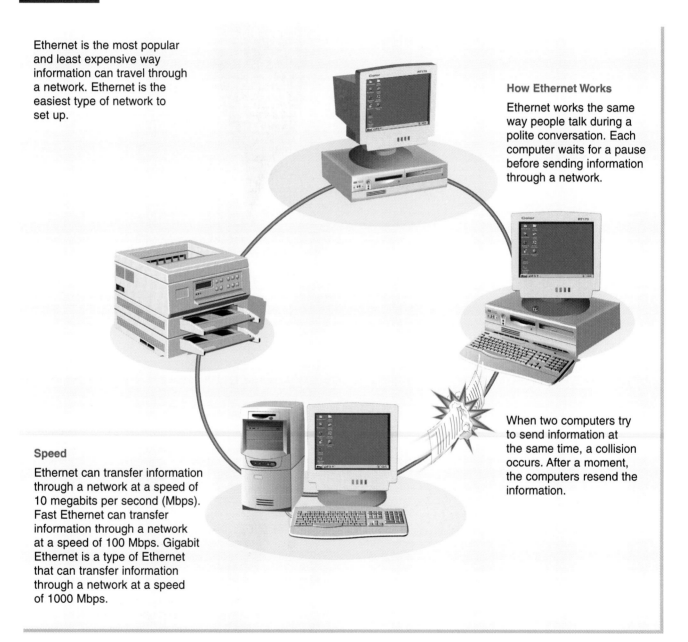

How Ethernet Works

Ethernet works the same way people talk during a polite conversation. Each computer waits for a pause before sending information through a network.

When two computers try to send information at the same time, a collision occurs. After a moment, the computers resend the information.

Speed

Ethernet can transfer information through a network at a speed of 10 megabits per second (Mbps). Fast Ethernet can transfer information through a network at a speed of 100 Mbps. Gigabit Ethernet is a type of Ethernet that can transfer information through a network at a speed of 1000 Mbps.

TOKEN-RING

Token-ring is a type of network often found in large organizations, such as banks and insurance companies.

How Token-ring Works

Token-ring works by passing a single token from computer to computer. The token collects and delivers information as it travels around the network.

Speed

A token-ring network can send information through a network at speeds of 4 or 16 Mbps.

ATM

Asynchronous Transfer Mode (ATM) is a faster and more efficient way to exchange large volumes of information on busy networks.

Companies often use ATM to transfer information between two separate networks.

How ATM Works

ATM works by sending information in equal-sized pieces, called cells.

Speed

ATM can send information at speeds of 25, 155, 622 or 2488 Mbps.

NETWORK SECURITY

FIREWALL

A firewall is special software or hardware designed to protect a private computer network from viruses and unauthorized access. Corporations, banks and research facilities use firewalls to keep information private and secure.

USER NAME AND PASSWORD

You usually have to enter a user name and password when you want to access information on a network. This ensures that only authorized people can use the information stored on the network.

Choose a Password

When choosing a password, do not use words that people can easily associate with you, such as your name or favorite sport. The most effective password connects two words or number sequences with a special character (example: easy@123). To increase security, memorize your password and do not write it down.

INTRANET

An intranet is a small version of the Internet within a company or organization.

DISTRIBUTE INFORMATION

An intranet is a very efficient and inexpensive way to make internal company documents available to employees. Companies use intranets to distribute information such as phone directories, product listings and job openings.

CONNECTED DOCUMENTS

Documents on an intranet are connected. Employees can select highlighted text or images, called hyperlinks or links, in one document to display a related document.

SOFTWARE

The software used to exchange information on an intranet, such as a Web browser or e-mail program, is the same as the software used to exchange information on the Internet.

CHAPTER 10

The Internet

What is the Internet and how can I get connected? This chapter will help you start exploring the Internet.

INTRODUCTION TO THE INTERNET

The Internet is the largest computer network in the world.

The Internet is often called the Net, the Information Superhighway or Cyberspace.

More than 350 million people throughout the world use the Internet today.

In the late 1960s, the U.S. Defense Department began the Internet. The network quickly grew to include scientists and researchers across the country and eventually included schools, businesses, organizations and individuals around the world.

The Internet consists of thousands of connected networks around the world. A network is a collection of computers that are connected to share information.

If part of the Internet fails, information finds a new route around the disabled computers.

FREE INFORMATION

Most of the information on the Internet is free. Governments, universities, colleges, companies and individuals provide free information to educate and entertain the public.

Each government agency, company and organization on the Internet is responsible for maintaining its own network on the Internet. When you transfer information over the Internet, these organizations allow the information to pass through their networks free of charge. This lets you avoid long distance charges.

WHAT THE INTERNET OFFERS

ELECTRONIC MAIL

Electronic mail (e-mail) is the most popular feature on the Internet. You can exchange electronic mail with people around the world, including friends, colleagues, family members, customers and even people you meet on the Internet. Electronic mail is fast, easy, inexpensive and saves paper.

INFORMATION

The Internet gives you access to information on any subject imaginable. This makes the Internet a valuable research tool. You can review newspapers, magazines, academic papers, dictionaries, encyclopedias, travel guides, government documents, television show transcripts, recipes, job listings, airline schedules and much more.

ENTERTAINMENT

The Internet offers many different forms of entertainment, such as radio broadcasts, video clips and music. You can find pictures from the latest films, watch live interviews with your favorite celebrities and listen to music before it is available in stores. You can also play interactive games with other people around the world.

DISCUSSION GROUPS

You can join discussion groups on the Internet to meet people around the world with similar interests. You can ask questions, discuss problems and read interesting stories. There are thousands of discussion groups on topics such as the environment, food, humor, music, politics and sports.

MESSAGING

You can use a chat or instant messaging program to exchange typed messages with another person on the Internet. A message you send will instantly appear on the other person's computer. You can have an online conversation with one person at a time or with a group of people.

PROGRAMS

You can find programs to use on your computer, including word processors, drawing programs and games. You can also obtain programs, called shareware, that you can try for a limited time. If you like the program and want to continue using it, you must pay the author of the program.

ONLINE SHOPPING

You can order goods and services on the Internet without leaving your desk. You can purchase items such as books, computer programs, flowers, music CDs, stocks and used cars.

HOW INFORMATION TRANSFERS

All computers on the Internet work together to transfer information around the world.

Packets

When you send information over the Internet, the information is broken down into smaller pieces, called packets. Each packet travels independently over the Internet and may take a different path to arrive at the intended destination. When information arrives at its destination, the packets are reassembled.

TCP/IP

Transmission Control Protocol/Internet Protocol (TCP/IP) is a language computers on the Internet use to communicate with each other. TCP/IP divides information you send into packets and sends the packets over the Internet. When information arrives at the intended destination, TCP/IP ensures that all the packets arrived safely.

Backbone

The backbone of the Internet consists of high-speed data lines that join major networks all over the world.

Router

A router is a specialized device that regulates traffic on the Internet and picks the most efficient route for each packet. A packet may pass through many routers before reaching its intended destination.

Sunkist

Download/Upload Information

When you receive information from another computer on the Internet, you are downloading the information.

When you send information to another computer on the Internet, you are uploading the information.

GETTING CONNECTED

You need equipment, software and an Internet service provider to connect to the Internet.

COMPUTER

You can use any type of computer, such as an IBM-compatible or Macintosh computer, to connect to the Internet.

SOFTWARE

Most computers come with software to help you set up the computer to access the Internet. For example, computers that come with Windows Me include the Internet Connection Wizard.

You also need software, such as a Web browser, to access information on the Internet. Most new computers come with this software installed.

MODEM OR HIGH-SPEED CONNECTION

You need a modem or high-speed Internet connection to connect to the Internet. For more information, see pages 52 to 57.

INTERNET SERVICE PROVIDER

An Internet Service Provider (ISP) is a company that gives you access to the Internet for a fee. Make sure you choose an ISP with a local telephone number to avoid long distance charges.

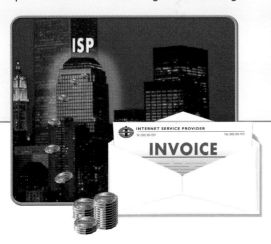

Commercial Online Service

A commercial online service is a type of ISP that offers an enormous amount of well-organized information and services such as daily news, weather reports and chat rooms. America Online (AOL) is the most popular commercial online service.

OTHER WAYS TO CONNECT

You can use some wireless devices, such as cellular telephones and handheld computers, to connect to the Internet so you can access information and exchange electronic mail.

There are also Internet television terminals that allow you to access the Internet using your television. An Internet television terminal is also called a set-top box.

CHOOSE AN INTERNET SERVICE PROVIDER

An Internet Service Provider (ISP) is a company that gives you access to the Internet. There are several factors you should consider when choosing an ISP.

TECHNICAL SUPPORT

You may encounter problems while setting up a connection to an ISP. The service provider you choose should have a technical support department to answer your questions. Find out if the ISP offers 24-hour telephone technical support to ensure that you will be able to contact the department on evenings and weekends, as well as during business hours.

ACCESS NUMBERS

Most ISPs let you connect to the Internet by dialing a local telephone number. Some service providers also have a toll free number you can use to connect to the Internet without having to pay long distance charges, even when you are traveling.

COST

There are different ways an ISP can charge you for the time you spend on the Internet. Many service providers offer a certain number of hours per month for a set fee. If you exceed the total number of hours, you are usually charged for every extra hour.

Some ISPs offer unlimited access to the Internet for a set fee. This is useful if you plan to frequently use the Internet. Make sure you are aware of any hidden charges.

TRIAL PERIOD

Some ISPs allow potential customers to use their service free of charge for a limited time. This allows you to fully evaluate the service provider before paying for the service.

DISCOUNTS

You should find out if the ISP you are considering offers any discounts. Some service providers offer a discount if you make automatic payments using your credit card or if you pay for an entire year instead of paying each month.

CHOOSE AN INTERNET SERVICE PROVIDER

RELIABILITY

If you plan to use a modem to connect to a service provider, ask the ISP how often users get a busy signal when trying to connect during the most popular connection times, such as evenings and weekends. If you hear a busy signal when you try to connect, you cannot access the Internet at that time.

CUSTOMER REFERENCES

You may want to ask an ISP for customer references that you can contact. You should also ask friends, relatives and colleagues who live in your area which service provider they use and if they are happy with the service.

TYPE OF CONNECTION

The ISP you choose must offer the type of connection you want to use to access the Internet. For example, if you want to use a high-speed cable modem connection, you will need an ISP that offers cable modem service.

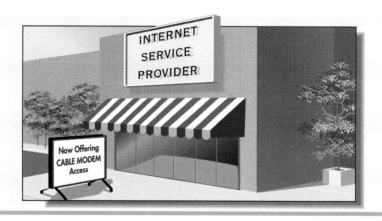

SOFTWARE

Most ISPs offer free software that lets you access information on the Internet. This software usually includes a Web browser and an e-mail program. The service provider should provide clear instructions on how to set up and use the software.

MULTIPLE E-MAIL ADDRESSES

Many ISPs allow you to have multiple e-mail addresses for one Internet account. This is useful if you want each member of your family to have their own e-mail address.

WEB PAGE PUBLISHING

You can create Web pages to share business or personal information with people around the world. Most ISPs offer space on their Web servers where you can publish your Web pages for free. Many service providers also provide software to help you create your Web pages.

FAMILY SERVICES

Some ISPs offer a service that can block access to offensive or illegal information on the Internet for you. If you are concerned about the type of information your family has access to on the Internet, you should find out if the service provider can block information.

CHAPTER 11

The World Wide Web

How do I browse the World Wide Web? This chapter introduces you to the Web and what it has to offer.

INTRODUCTION TO THE WEB

The World Wide Web is part of the Internet and consists of a huge collection of documents stored on computers around the world.

The World Wide Web is commonly known as the Web.

Web Page

A Web page is a document on the Web. Web pages can include text, images, sound and video.

Web Server

A Web server is a computer on the Internet that stores Web pages. Once a Web page is stored on a Web server, it is available for other people to view.

Popular Web Sites

Some Web sites are popular and can get very busy. You may find that it takes longer to view the information on a busy Web site. If it is taking a long time to view a Web site, try connecting again later.

Web Site

A Web site is a collection of Web pages maintained by a college, university, government agency, company or individual.

URL

Each Web page has a unique address, called a Uniform Resource Locator (URL). You can instantly display any Web page if you know its URL.

A Web page URL starts with **http** (HyperText Transfer Protocol) and contains the **computer name**, **directory name** and the **name of the Web page**.

HYPERLINKS

Web pages contain highlighted text or images, called hyperlinks or links, that connect to other pages on the Web. Hyperlinks allow you to easily move through a vast amount of information by jumping from one Web page to another. You can select a hyperlink to jump to a Web page located on the same computer or a computer across the city, country or world.

You can easily identify text hyperlinks on a Web page because they appear underlined and in color.

WEB BROWSER

A Web browser is a program that lets you view and explore information on the World Wide Web.

Most Web browsers have a similar look and feel.

This area displays a toolbar to help you quickly perform common tasks.

This area displays the address of the page you are currently viewing.

This area displays a Web page.

POPULAR WEB BROWSERS

Microsoft Internet Explorer

Microsoft Internet Explorer is currently the most popular Web browser. Internet Explorer comes with most versions of the Windows operating system and with the latest version of the Macintosh operating system.

You can also obtain Internet Explorer free of charge at www.microsoft.com/windows/ie.

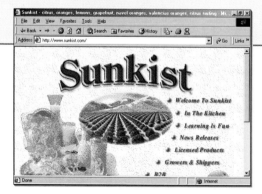

Netscape Navigator

Netscape Navigator is a Web browser that is available as a separate program or as part of the Netscape Communicator suite, which also includes several other Internet-related programs.

You can obtain Netscape Navigator free of charge at www.netscape.com.

WEB BROWSER FEATURES

Home Page

The home page is the Web page that appears each time you start your Web browser.

You can choose any page on the Web as your home page. You should choose a home page that provides a good starting point for exploring the Web.

Bookmarks

Most Web browsers have a feature, called bookmarks or favorites, that lets you store the addresses of Web pages you frequently visit. Bookmarks save you from having to remember and constantly retype your favorite Web page addresses.

History List

When you are browsing through pages on the World Wide Web, it can be difficult to keep track of the locations of pages you have visited. Most Web browsers include a history list that allows you to quickly return to Web pages you have recently visited.

Navigation Buttons

Most Web browsers provide buttons that help you move through information on the Web. These buttons allow you to move backward and forward through Web pages you have viewed, display your home page and stop the transfer of a Web page.

SEARCH TOOL

There are many free services you can use to find information on the Web. These services are called search tools.

A search tool catalogs Web pages to make them easier to find.

POPULAR SEARCH TOOLS

You can find popular search tools at the following Web sites:

ragingsearch.com

www.google.com

www.askjeeves.com

Web portals also offer search tools. For more information on Web portals, see page 212.

SEARCH USING WEB BROWSER

Most new Web browsers allow you to quickly search for information on the Web. Instead of typing a Web page address in your Web browser, you may be able to type a word or phrase you want to search for. The Web browser will display a list of hyperlinks to Web pages containing the word or phrase you entered. You can click one of the hyperlinks to view the Web page.

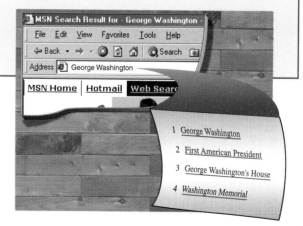

HOW SEARCH TOOLS FIND INFORMATION

Most search tools use programs, called robots or spiders, to find new and updated pages on the Web. People can also submit information about Web pages they have created to search tools.

Since hundreds of new Web pages are created each day, it is impossible for search tools to catalog every new page on the Web.

WEB SITE REVIEWS

Some search tools have people who review and catalog each new Web page. These people group Web sites containing similar information together in categories to make it easier for you to find the information you want.

When people review Web sites for a search tool, they also examine the quality of information in the Web sites and may rate the Web sites to help you narrow your search.

AVAILABLE WEB PAGES

Just as many new Web pages are created each day, many pages are removed from the Web each day. When you use a search tool to find information on the Web, some of the Web pages may have moved or no longer exist. A good search tool checks Web pages frequently to make sure the pages still exist.

WEB PORTAL

A Web portal is a Web site that provides an excellent starting point for exploring the Internet.

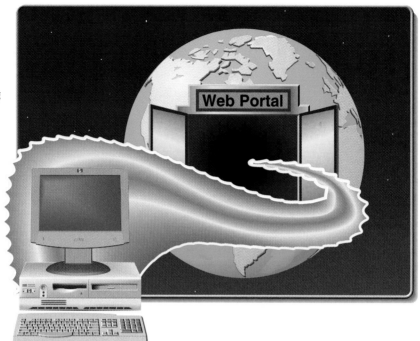

Web Portal

You can find popular Web portals at the following Web sites:

www.excite.com

www.go.com

www.lycos.com

www.yahoo.com

FIND INFORMATION

Web portals allow you to browse through categories, such as business or sports, to find information that interests you. Web portals also let you type a word or phrase to quickly search for information on the Web.

NEWS

Most Web portals provide a variety of up-to-date news headlines, as well as sports scores, weather forecasts and stock quotes. You can select a news headline to read a full article about the news item.

SHOPPING

Many Web portals provide access to online shopping. You can buy items such as clothing, sports equipment, books and gardening tools.

FREE E-MAIL

Web portals usually offer free e-mail services, which allow you to send and receive e-mail from any computer that has access to the Web.

CHAT

Web portals often offer chat services that allow you to instantly communicate with people around the world.

PEOPLE SEARCH

Most Web portals allow you to search for a person's telephone number and address. Many Web portals also let you search for a person's e-mail address.

MAPS

Many Web portals offer maps and driving directions. For example, you can find the distance and best route between two addresses.

GAMES

Most Web portals allow you to play games, such as chess or crossword puzzles. You can play against the computer or against other people visiting the portal.

CUSTOMIZE

You can customize many Web portals to display the information you want. For example, you could customize a Web portal to display the weather forecast for your area.

MULTIMEDIA ON THE WEB

Web pages commonly use multimedia—a combination of text, images, sound and video or animation—to entertain visitors and attract attention to information.

TRANSFER TIME

Some multimedia files take a long time to transfer to a computer. A Web page usually shows the size of a file to give you an indication of how long the file will take to transfer.

	File Size		Time
Bytes	Kilobytes (KB)	Megabytes (MB)	(estimated)
10,000,000	10,000	10	25 minutes
5,000,000	5,000	5	12 minutes
2,500,000	2,500	2.5	8 minutes

The speed of your Internet connection and the size of the multimedia file affect how long the file will take to transfer. Some large files, such as videos, may take a long time to transfer even if you use a high-speed Internet connection.

WEB BROWSER PLUG-INS

Some Web browsers need special programs, called plug-ins, to display or play certain types of multimedia files on the Web. A plug-in adds features to a Web browser. If your Web browser does not have the necessary plug-in, the browser may prompt you to install the plug-in.

STREAMING MULTIMEDIA

Streaming multimedia is a system that lets you hear or view continuous sound or video on the Web, such as a live concert or sporting event.

You must have a streaming multimedia player to play streaming multimedia on the Web. You can find streaming multimedia players at the following Web sites:

RealPlayer

www.real.com

QuickTime

www.apple.com/quicktime

WEB PAGE ENHANCEMENTS

Most new Web browsers can display Java, JavaScript and ActiveX enhancements.

Java

Java is a complex programming language that allows people to create animated and interactive Web pages. Java-enhanced Web pages can display animation and moving text, play music and much more.

JavaScript

JavaScript is a simple programming language that is used mainly for Web page enhancements, such as displaying scrolling messages and fading-in Web pages.

ActiveX

ActiveX is a technology used to improve Web pages. For example, people can use ActiveX to add pop-up menus that instantly display a list of options on a Web page.

MP3

MP3 is a sound format used to transfer CD-quality music over the Internet.

MP3 stands for Motion Picture Experts Group Audio Layer 3.

MP3 FORMAT

The MP3 format compresses sound files so they take up small amounts of disk space. The small size of MP3 files allows the files to transfer quickly and easily over the Internet.

DOWNLOAD MP3 FILES

Some recording artists distribute their music in MP3 format on the Web to promote their music. There are many Web sites that allow you to download, or copy, individual songs or entire CDs in MP3 format to your computer. Some sites offer the music for free and some require you to purchase the music. You can find MP3 files at the following Web sites:

www.emusic.com   www.riffage.com
www.mp3.com

USING MP3

MP3 Player

You can install special software, called an MP3 player, on your computer to download and play MP3 files. Some MP3 players look and act like a CD player. They have play, pause and stop buttons, as well as balance, volume and equalizer controls.

You can find MP3 players at the following Web sites:

Winamp (Windows)
www.winamp.com

Unsanity Echo (Macintosh)
www.unsanity.com

Some operating systems come with media player software that can play MP3 files. For example, the Windows Media Player program included with Windows Me can play MP3 files.

Create Your Own CDs

If you have a CD-R (CD-Recordable) or CD-RW (CD-ReWritable) drive and the appropriate software, you can create your own CDs using MP3 files you have downloaded. If your CD-R or CD-RW drive did not come with the necessary software, you can obtain software on the Web. For example, Nero by Ahead Software is available at the www.nero.com Web site.

SHOPPING ON THE WEB

You can buy products and services on the Web without ever leaving your desk.

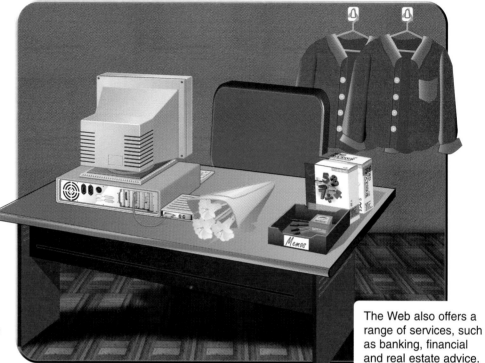

There are thousands of products you can buy on the Web, such as clothing, office supplies and computer programs. The Web is also a great source for purchasing rare items, such as out-of-print books.

The Web also offers a range of services, such as banking, financial and real estate advice.

COMPANIES

Many companies have Web sites where you can view and buy their products. There are also Web sites that offer a variety of products from many different companies. For example, you can find products such as lawn furniture, kitchen accessories, books and video games at www.walmart.com.

AUCTIONS

You can find auctions on the Web that allow you to bid on products such as computers, jewelry, gifts and much more. One of the most popular auction Web sites, eBay, is located at www.ebay.com.

SHOPPING CONSIDERATIONS

Secure Web Sites

Security is important when you want to send confidential information, such as credit card numbers and bank records, over the Internet. You can safely transfer confidential information to a secure Web site. The address of a secure Web site usually starts with https rather than http.

Delivery

When you buy a product on the Web, you can usually have the product delivered to your door. Most companies charge for delivery, so make sure you consider the delivery charges before ordering.

ADVANTAGES OF SHOPPING ON THE WEB

Up-to-date Information

Most Web sites offer more up-to-date information about products and prices than catalogs and flyers. Before buying a product, you can find the latest reviews and ratings of the product on the Web.

Low Prices

The prices of products sold on the Web are generally lower than prices in traditional stores, since companies do not have overhead costs, such as rent and salespeople. Many stores on the Web also give discounts when you make a purchase.

CHILDREN AND THE WEB

Children should be carefully monitored when browsing the World Wide Web.

Most of the information on the Web is meant to educate or entertain people, but some sites may contain material that is inappropriate for children.

TYPES OF INAPPROPRIATE INFORMATION

Pictures

There are many sites on the Web that display pictures meant for adult users. Most adult-oriented sites require verification that users are adults, but the sites often display sample pictures on the first page of the Web site.

Documents

There are many documents on the Web describing everything from causing mischief at school to making explosives. These types of documents may appeal to teenagers and may be found at Web sites distributing banned or censored books. These Web sites generally do not have any restrictions on who can access the documents.

HOW TO RESTRICT ACCESS

Adult Supervision

Constant adult supervision is the best way to ensure that children do not access inappropriate information on the Web.

Ground Rules

• No foul language

• No X-rated Web sites

• Do not give personal information to strangers

Before each Web browsing session, the adult and child should decide on the purpose of the session, such as researching a school project. This will help set ground rules for browsing and make the time spent on the Web more productive.

Browser Restrictions

Some Web browsers allow you to restrict the information children can access on the Web. Many Web sites are rated using a system similar to the one used to rate television shows and films.

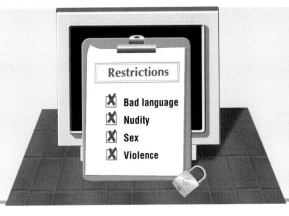

Restrictions

☒ Bad language

☒ Nudity

☒ Sex

☒ Violence

You can set your Web browser to allow access only to Web sites that comply with specific ratings.

Restriction Programs

You can buy programs that let you restrict access to certain Web sites. Most of these programs provide a frequently updated list of Web sites considered inappropriate for children.

You can purchase restriction programs at the following Web sites:

Cyber Patrol
www.cyberpatrol.com

Net Nanny
www.netnanny.com

CREATE AND PUBLISH WEB PAGES

You can create and publish Web pages to share information with people around the world.

Individuals publish Web pages to share their favorite pictures, hobbies and interests. Companies publish Web pages to promote their businesses, advertise products and publicize job openings.

ORGANIZE IDEAS

Before you start creating Web pages, decide what ideas you will discuss and how the ideas relate to one another. Break up your information so you discuss one major idea on each Web page. You may find it helpful to first sketch the design of your Web pages on paper.

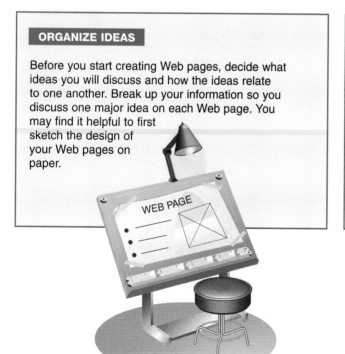

HTML

HyperText Markup Language (HTML) is a computer code used to create Web pages. There are many programs available, called visual editors, which can help you create Web pages without having to learn HTML. You can obtain visual editors at the following Web sites:

Microsoft FrontPage
www.microsoft.com/frontpage

HoTMetaL PRO
www.softquad.com

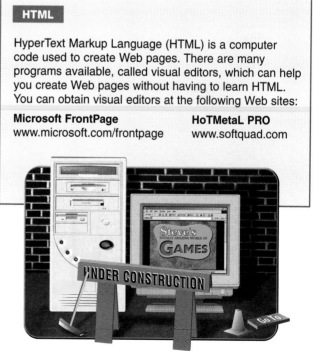

HYPERLINKS

You can add hyperlinks, or links, to your Web pages. Hyperlinks are highlighted text or images that connect to other pages on the Web. Hyperlinks are one of the most important features of Web pages since they let people move easily through information of interest.

IMAGES

You can add images to your Web pages to enhance the appearance of the pages. You can create your own images, use a scanner to scan images into your computer, buy images at computer stores or find images on the Internet. Make sure you have permission to use any images you did not create yourself.

PUBLISH YOUR WEB PAGES

When you finish creating your Web pages, you can publish the pages by transferring them to a Web server. The company that gives you access to the Internet usually offers space on its Web server where you can publish your Web pages.

CHAPTER 12

Electronic Mail and Mailing Lists

How can I communicate with other people on the Internet? This chapter introduces you to electronic mail and mailing lists.

INTRODUCTION TO E-MAIL

You can exchange electronic mail (e-mail) with people around the world.

E-mail is a fast, economical and convenient way to send messages to family, friends and colleagues.

E-MAIL PROGRAMS

An e-mail program lets you send, receive and manage your e-mail messages.

Popular e-mail programs include Microsoft Outlook Express, Netscape Messenger and Qualcomm's Eudora.

■ This area displays the folders that contain your e-mail messages.

■ This area displays the contents of a single e-mail message.

■ This area displays a list of all your e-mail messages.

■ This area displays a list of your contacts.

E-MAIL ADVANTAGES

Speed

E-mail is much faster than old-fashioned mail, which is sometimes called "snail mail." An e-mail message can travel around the world in minutes.

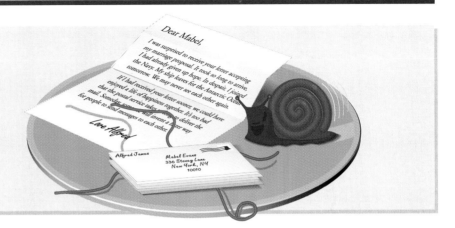

Cost

Once you pay a service provider for a connection to the Internet, there is no charge for sending and receiving e-mail. You do not have to pay extra even if you send a long message or if the message travels around the world.

Exchanging e-mail can save you money on long distance calls. The next time you are about to pick up the telephone, consider sending an e-mail message instead.

Convenience

You can create and send e-mail messages at any time. The person receiving the message does not have to be at their computer when you send the message. E-mail makes communicating with people in different time zones very convenient.

E-MAIL ADDRESSES

You can send a message to anyone around the world if you know the person's e-mail address.

An e-mail address defines the location of an individual's mailbox on the Internet.

PARTS OF AN E-MAIL ADDRESS

An e-mail address consists of two parts separated by the @ ("at") symbol. An e-mail address cannot contain spaces.

The **user name** is the name of the person's account. This can be a real name or a nickname.

The **domain name** is the location of the person's account on the Internet. Periods (.) separate the various parts of the domain name.

ORGANIZATION OR COUNTRY

The last few characters in an e-mail address usually indicate the type of organization the person belongs to or the country the person lives in.

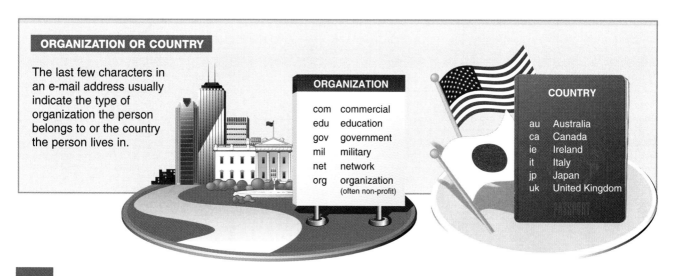

ORGANIZATION	
com	commercial
edu	education
gov	government
mil	military
net	network
org	organization (often non-profit)

COUNTRY	
au	Australia
ca	Canada
ie	Ireland
it	Italy
jp	Japan
uk	United Kingdom

BOUNCED MESSAGES

A bounced message is a message that returns to you because it cannot reach its destination. A message usually bounces because of typing mistakes in the e-mail address.

Before sending a message, make sure you check the e-mail address for accuracy.

ADDRESS BOOK

Most e-mail programs provide an address book where you can store the addresses of people you frequently send messages to. An address book saves you from having to type the same addresses over and over again.

FIND E-MAIL ADDRESSES

The best way to find the e-mail address of a friend or colleague is to ask the person for their address. Although there is no central listing of e-mail addresses, there are many places on the Web that can help you search for e-mail addresses.

You can search for e-mail addresses at the following Web sites:

people.yahoo.com

www.bigfoot.com

SEND A MESSAGE

You can send a message to exchange ideas or request information.

When you send a message, do not assume the person will read the message right away. Some people may not regularly check their messages.

If you want to practice sending a message, send a message to yourself.

Make sure every message you send is clear, concise and contains no spelling or grammar errors. Also make sure the message will not be misinterpreted. For example, the reader may not realize a statement is meant to be sarcastic.

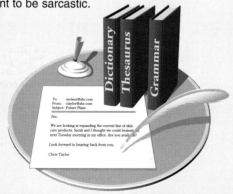

You can have an e-mail program add information about yourself to the end of every message you send. This prevents you from having to repeatedly type the same information.

A signature can include your name, e-mail address, occupation or favorite quotation. You can also use plain characters to display simple pictures.

SMILEYS

You can use special characters, called smileys or emoticons, to express emotions in messages. These characters resemble human faces if you turn them sideways.

SMILEYS

Gesture	Characters
Cry	:'-(
Frown	:-(
Indifferent	:-I
Laugh	:-D
Smile	:-)
Surprise	:-0
Wink	;-)

ABBREVIATIONS

Abbreviations are commonly used in messages to save time typing.

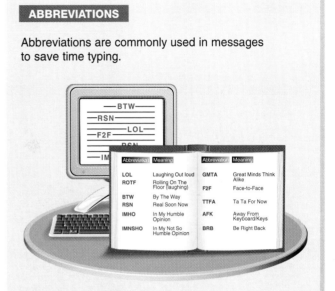

Abbreviation	Meaning
LOL	Laughing Out loud
ROTF	Rolling On The Floor (laughing)
BTW	By The Way
RSN	Real Soon Now
IMHO	In My Humble Opinion
IMNSHO	In My Not So Humble Opinion

Abbreviation	Meaning
GMTA	Great Minds Think Alike
F2F	Face-to-Face
TTFA	Ta Ta For Now
AFK	Away From Keyboard/Keys
BRB	Be Right Back

SHOUTING

A MESSAGE WRITTEN IN CAPITAL LETTERS IS ANNOYING AND HARD TO READ. THIS IS CALLED SHOUTING.

Always use uppercase and lowercase letters when typing messages.

FLAME

A flame is an angry or insulting message directed at one person. A flame war is an argument that continues for a while. Avoid starting or participating in flame wars.

RECEIVE A MESSAGE

Your computer does not have to be turned on to receive an e-mail message. Your Internet service provider stores the messages you receive in a mailbox. When you check for new messages, you are checking your mailbox on the service provider's computer. Make sure you regularly check for messages.

You can use most computers on the Internet to connect to your service provider and retrieve your messages. This allows you to check your messages while traveling.

AUTOMATICALLY CHECK FOR MESSAGES

Most e-mail programs automatically check for new e-mail messages. You can specify how often you want the program to check for new messages.

You may want to have your e-mail program check for messages approximately every 30 minutes. If your e-mail program is constantly checking for new messages, it can slow down the performance of other tasks, such as browsing the Web.

REPLY TO A MESSAGE

You can reply to a message to answer a question, express an opinion or supply additional information.

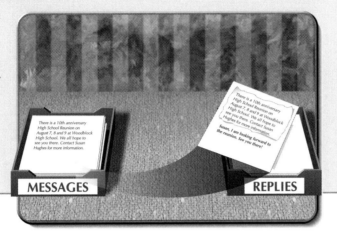

MESSAGES

REPLIES

Quoting

When you reply to a message, make sure you include part of the original message. This is called quoting. Quoting helps the reader identify which message you are replying to. To save the reader time, make sure you delete all parts of the original message that do not directly relate to your reply.

FORWARD A MESSAGE

After reading a message, you can add comments and then send the message to a friend or colleague.

There is a 10th anniversary High School Reunion on August 8, 9 and 10 at Woodblock High School. We all hope to see you there. Contact Susan Hughes for more information.

Rick, I thought you might be interested in the reunion. Unfortunately, I will be out of town.

FORWARD TO:
Rick M.

ATTACH A FILE TO A MESSAGE

You can attach a document, picture, sound, video or program to a message you are sending. The computer receiving the message must have a program that can display or play the file.

You should try to keep the size of an attached file under 500 KB, since many computers on the Internet take a long time to transfer messages with large attached files.

WEB-BASED E-MAIL

There are several Web sites that allow you to send and receive e-mail on the Web free of charge.

You use your Web browser to send and receive Web-based e-mail. You do not need an e-mail program installed on your computer.

POPULAR WEB-BASED E-MAIL SERVICES

There are several Web-based e-mail services available. You can find popular Web-based e-mail services at the following Web sites:

www.hotmail.com
www.email.com
mail.yahoo.com

WORLDWIDE ACCESS

When you use a Web-based e-mail service, you can access your e-mail from any computer in the world that has access to the Web. Web-based e-mail is useful for people who need to access their e-mail while traveling.

PERMANENT E-MAIL ADDRESS

Using a Web-based e-mail service allows you to obtain an e-mail address that will not change. This lets you keep the same e-mail address even if you switch to a new Internet service provider.

E-MAIL VIRUSES

An e-mail virus is a program that can disrupt the normal operation of a computer.

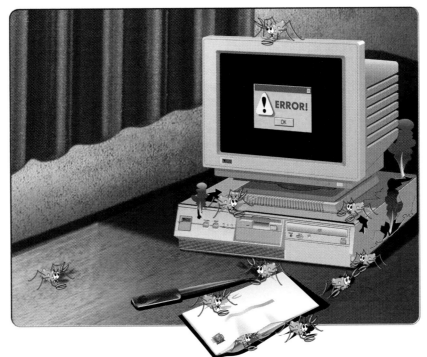

A virus can cause problems such as displaying unusual messages on the screen or destroying information on the hard drive.

HOW E-MAIL VIRUSES SPREAD

Most e-mail viruses spread to your computer when you open an e-mail attachment containing the virus. You can spread some e-mail viruses to your computer just by opening an infected e-mail message. A virus can spread to other computers if you forward a message containing the virus to other people. Some e-mail viruses can also access your address book and send themselves to the e-mail addresses stored there.

VIRUS PREVENTION

Only open e-mail attachments and e-mail messages sent by people you trust. You should also use a virus scanner program to check e-mail messages for viruses. Virus scanner manufacturers regularly release updates that allow their programs to detect the latest known viruses. Make sure your virus scanner is up-to-date.

You can find popular virus scanner programs at the following Web sites:

www.mcafee.com
www.symantec.com/nav

A mailing list is a discussion group that uses e-mail to communicate. When a mailing list receives a message, a copy of the message is sent to everyone on the mailing list.

There are thousands of mailing lists that cover a wide variety of topics, from aromatherapy to zoology.

You can find mailing lists at the following Web sites:

paml.net

www.liszt.com

SUBSCRIBE TO A MAILING LIST

Just as you would subscribe to a newspaper or magazine, you can subscribe to a mailing list that interests you. Subscribing adds your e-mail address to the mailing list.

After you subscribe to a mailing list, make sure you check your e-mail frequently. You can receive dozens of messages in a short period of time.

Unsubscribe

If you no longer want to receive messages from a mailing list, you can unsubscribe from the mailing list at any time. Unsubscribing removes your e-mail address from the mailing list.

MAILING LIST ADDRESSES

Each mailing list has two addresses. Make sure you send your messages to the appropriate address.

Mailing List Address

The mailing list address receives messages intended for the entire mailing list. This is the address you use to send messages you want all the people on the list to receive. Do not send subscription or unsubscription requests to the mailing list address.

Administrative Address

The administrative address receives messages dealing with administrative issues. This is the address you use to subscribe to or unsubscribe from a mailing list.

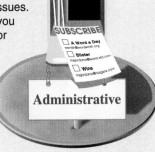

MANUALLY MAINTAINED LISTS

A manually maintained list is managed by a person, who is often referred to as an administrator.

Before you subscribe to a manually maintained list, make sure you find out what information the administrator needs and include the information in your message.

AUTOMATED LISTS

An automated mailing list is managed by a computer program. The three most popular programs for managing automated mailing lists are listproc, listserv and majordomo.

The name of the program that manages the mailing list usually appears in the e-mail address you use to subscribe to the list (example: listserv@LSV.UKY.EDU).

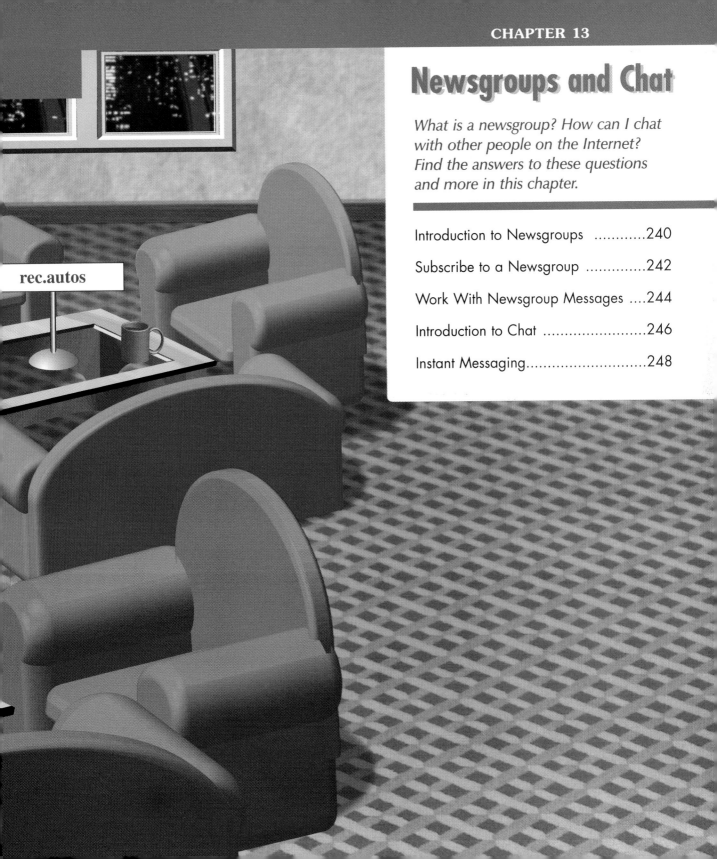

CHAPTER 13

Newsgroups and Chat

What is a newsgroup? How can I chat with other people on the Internet? Find the answers to these questions and more in this chapter.

rec.autos

INTRODUCTION TO NEWSGROUPS

A newsgroup is a discussion group that allows people with common interests to communicate with each other.

There are thousands of newsgroups on every subject imaginable. Each newsgroup discusses a particular topic such as jobs offered, puzzles or medicine.

Usenet, short for Users' Network, refers to all the computers that distribute newsgroup information.

NEWSGROUP NAMES

The name of a newsgroup describes the type of information discussed in the newsgroup. A newsgroup name consists of two or more words, separated by periods (.).

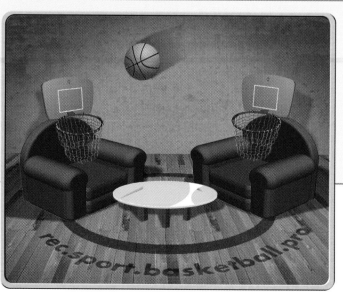

The first word describes the main topic (example: rec for recreation). Each of the following words narrows the topic.

MESSAGES

A newsgroup can contain hundreds or thousands of messages.

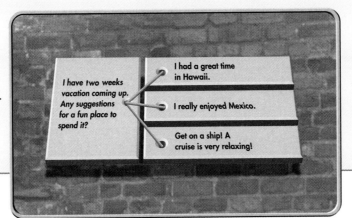

Message

A message is information that an individual posts, or sends, to a newsgroup. A message can be a few lines of text or the length of a book. Messages are also called articles.

Thread

A thread is a message and all replies to the message. A thread may include an initial question and the responses from other readers.

NEWSREADER

A newsreader is a program that lets you read and post messages to newsgroups. Microsoft Outlook Express comes with a built-in newsreader. Other popular newsreaders include MicroPlanet Gravity and Forté Free Agent.

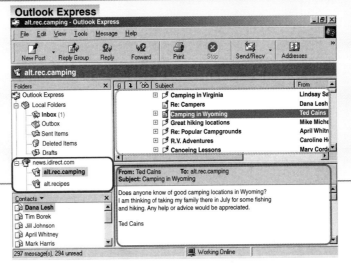

■ This area displays a list of newsgroups.

▨ This area displays a list of all the messages in the selected newsgroup.

■ This area displays the contents of a single message.

SUBSCRIBE TO A NEWSGROUP

You can subscribe to a newsgroup you want to read on a regular basis.

If you no longer want to read the messages in a newsgroup, you can unsubscribe from the newsgroup at any time.

NEWSGROUP CATEGORIES

Newsgroups are divided into sections, or categories. The newsgroups in each category discuss the same general topic.

Main Newsgroup Categories

Category	Topic	Example
alt	General interest	alt.fan.actors
biz	Business	biz.entrepreneurs
comp	Computers	comp.security.misc
misc	Miscellaneous	misc.books.technical
rec	Recreation and hobbies	rec.food.recipes
sci	Science	sci.physics
soc	Social (culture and politics)	soc.history
talk	Debate	talk.politics.misc

You can also find newsgroup categories that focus on specific subjects, such as companies or geographic locations. For example, you can find newsgroups that discuss only Microsoft products (example: microsoft.public.office.misc) or newsgroups that discuss issues about your city or state (example: nyc.politics).

NEW NEWSGROUPS

New newsgroups are created every day. You can display a list of all the newsgroups that have been created since the last time you checked. Once you have the list of new newsgroups, you can subscribe to a new newsgroup of interest.

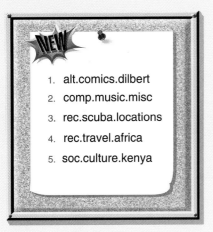

NEW

1. alt.comics.dilbert
2. comp.music.misc
3. rec.scuba.locations
4. rec.travel.africa
5. soc.culture.kenya

SIMILAR NEWSGROUPS

There is often more than one newsgroup for a topic. For example, the topics discussed in the **alt.books.reviews** newsgroup are similar to the topics discussed in **rec.arts.books**. If you are interested in a specific topic, you may want to subscribe to all the newsgroups that discuss the topic.

Similar Newsgroups

alt.autos
rec.autos
alt.cars

MODERATED NEWSGROUPS

Some newsgroups are moderated. In these newsgroups, a volunteer reads each message and decides if the message is appropriate for the newsgroup. The volunteer then posts the approved messages for everyone to read.

Moderated newsgroups may have the word "moderated" at the end of the newsgroup name (example: misc.taxes.moderated).

WORK WITH NEWSGROUP MESSAGES

POST A MESSAGE

You can post, or send, a new message to a newsgroup to ask a question or express an opinion. Thousands of people around the world may read a message you post.

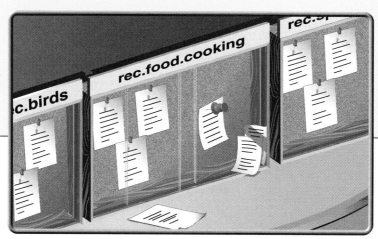

If you want to practice posting a message, send a message to the **alt.test** newsgroup. Do not send practice messages to other newsgroups.

REPLY TO A MESSAGE

You can reply to a message to answer a question, express an opinion or supply additional information. When you reply to a message, make sure you include part of the original message. This is called quoting. Quoting helps readers identify which message you are replying to.

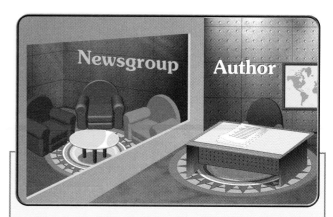

Send a Private Reply

You can send a reply to the author of a message, the entire newsgroup or both. If your reply would not be of interest to others in a newsgroup or if you want to send a private reply, send a message only to the author of the message.

MESSAGE CONSIDERATIONS

Read Messages Before Posting

You should read the messages in a newsgroup for approximately one week before posting a message. This is called lurking. Lurking is a good way to learn how people in a newsgroup communicate and prevents you from posting information others have already read.

Read the FAQ

The FAQ (Frequently Asked Questions) is a document containing a list of questions and answers that often appear in a newsgroup. The FAQ is designed to prevent new readers from asking questions that have already been answered. Make sure you read the newsgroup's FAQ before posting a message.

Post to the Appropriate Newsgroup

Make sure you post a message to the appropriate newsgroup. This ensures that people interested in your questions and comments will see your message.

Do not post an inappropriate message to multiple newsgroups. This is called spamming. Spamming is particularly annoying when the message serves a commercial purpose, such as selling a product or service.

INTRODUCTION TO CHAT

You can instantly communicate with people around the world by typing back and forth. This is called chatting.

Chatting is one of the most popular features of the Internet.

You can chat with family, friends and colleagues in other cities, states or countries without paying long distance telephone charges.

TEXT-BASED CHAT

Text-based chat is the oldest and most popular type of chat on the Internet. You can have conversations with one or more people. When chatting, the text you send immediately appears on the screen of each person participating in the conversation.

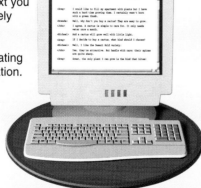

NICKNAMES

Many people choose nicknames rather than using their real names when chatting. Using a nickname helps protect your privacy.

If another person is already using a nickname you want, you must choose a different nickname.

INTERNET RELAY CHAT

Internet Relay Chat (IRC) is a popular chatting system on the Internet. You can join a chat group, or channel, on IRC. Each channel focuses on a specific topic, such as music or politics.

You need an IRC program to participate in IRC chats. You can obtain an IRC program at the www.mirc.com Web site.

WEB-BASED CHAT

There are sites on the Web that let you chat with other people. For example, the www.talkcity.com Web site offers Web-based chat. Usually, all you need to participate in Web-based chat is your Web browser.

MULTIMEDIA CHAT

Multimedia chat lets you have voice conversations and communicate through live video over the Internet. You need equipment such as a microphone, speakers and a video camera to participate in multimedia chat.

Since sound and video transfer over the Internet more slowly than text, you should have a high-speed connection to the Internet to use multimedia chat.

You need a special program to hear and see people while chatting on the Internet. For example, Microsoft NetMeeting is a popular multimedia chat program available at the www.microsoft.com/netmeeting Web site.

INSTANT MESSAGING

You can exchange instant messages to have a private conversation with a friend, colleague or family member on the Internet.

Brian Edwards>
How's the weather?
Andy Lemon>
It snowed again last night.

Brian Edwards>
How's the weather?
Andy Lemon>
It snowed again last night.

Each message you send will immediately appear on the other person's screen.

INSTANT MESSAGING PROGRAM

You need to install an instant messaging program on your computer to exchange instant messages with other people. You and the people you want to exchange messages with must use compatible instant messaging programs. You can find popular instant messaging programs at the following Web sites:

ICQ
www.icq.com

AOL Instant Messenger
www.aol.com/aim

MSN Messenger Service
messenger.msn.com

Contact List

Instant messaging programs provide a contact list where you can save the identities of people you frequently exchange messages with. After you add a person to your contact list, your instant messaging program will notify you when the person goes online.

REASONS FOR INSTANT MESSAGES

Save Money

Sending instant messages is a great way to communicate with family and friends around the world without paying long distance telephone charges. Once you pay a service provider for a connection to the Internet, there is no charge for sending and receiving instant messages.

Communicate With Colleagues

Sending instant messages is ideal for companies that have employees located in different offices or employees who work from home. Instant messaging programs allow employees to see when their colleagues are online and easily communicate with them. Using instant messages is more convenient than leaving phone messages.

Meet New People

You can meet people on the Internet who use an instant messaging program. When people register with an instant messaging program, they can enter information about themselves, such as their occupation, hobbies and interests. You can use this information to find and then communicate with people who share your interests.

CHAPTER 14

Multimedia Devices

What is a portable MP3 player? What should I look for when choosing a digital camera? Find the answers to these questions and more in this chapter.

A portable MP3 player is a device that stores MP3 music files so you can listen to the music when you are away from your computer.

MP3 is a sound format used to transfer CD-quality music over the Internet. MP3 stands for Motion Picture Experts Group Audio Layer 3. The MP3 format compresses sound files so they take up small amounts of disk space.

Popular portable MP3 players include S3's Rio and Creative Labs' Nomad Jukebox.

Most portable MP3 players are solid-state devices, which means they have no moving parts. This allows you to listen to music while you are jogging or exercising without worrying about the music skipping.

You can connect a portable MP3 player to your computer to transfer MP3 files from the computer to the player. Once you have transferred files to the MP3 player, you can disconnect the player from the computer.

MEMORY

Many portable MP3 players use flash memory, which is a type of memory that can be quickly erased and re-recorded. Flash memory can be built-in memory or a removable memory card that fits inside the MP3 player. MP3 players with flash memory commonly offer 64 MB of memory, which allows you to store up to an hour of high quality music.

Some portable MP3 players have built-in hard drives, providing more storage space. For example, Creative Labs' Nomad Jukebox has a 6 GB hard drive that can store up to 100 hours of music.

OBTAIN MP3 FILES

There are many companies on the Web, such as EMusic.com and MP3.com, that allow you to download, or copy, individual songs or entire CDs in the MP3 format to your computer. Some companies offer the music for free and some require you to purchase the music.

You can also obtain an MP3 encoder program, such as the MusicMatch Jukebox program, that allows you to convert the songs on a CD to the MP3 format.

DIGITAL CAMERA

A digital camera lets you take photos that you can use on your computer.

Most digital cameras come with image editing software that allows you to view and edit the photos on your computer.

WORK WITH PHOTOS

You can transfer photos from a digital camera to a computer. This lets you use the photos in documents, on the World Wide Web or in e-mail messages.

If you want prints of the photos you take, you can have a company such as Kodak develop the photos for a fee. You can also buy a color photo printer to print your own photos.

FEATURES

Most digital cameras come with a color Liquid Crystal Display (LCD) screen, which is the same type of display found in notebook computers. You can use the LCD screen to preview your shots and view photos you have taken.

Most digital cameras include a built-in flash. You may also want to look for other features such as a zoom lens and the ability to record short videos.

MEGAPIXELS

The quality of photos a digital camera can produce depends on the detail the camera can detect. This detail, or resolution, is measured in megapixels. One megapixel is equivalent to a resolution of approximately 1000 x 1000 pixels.

1-megapixel   3-megapixel

The higher the number of megapixels a camera can detect, the clearer and more detailed the photos. There are currently 1, 2 and 3-megapixel digital cameras available.

MEMORY

Digital cameras store photos in memory until you transfer the photos to your computer. Digital cameras can have removable or built-in memory.

Removable

Most digital cameras with removable memory store photos on a memory card. Some digital cameras store photos on a regular floppy disk that fits inside the camera. Once a memory card or floppy disk is full, you can replace the card or disk in the camera to continue storing photos.

Built-in

Once the memory in a digital camera with built-in memory is full, you must transfer the photos to your computer. You can then store new photos in the camera's memory.

WEB CAMERA

A Web camera is a device that allows you to send live videos over the Internet.

You can also use a Web camera to record videos that you can save on your computer.

VIDEOCONFERENCING

Web cameras are often used for videoconferencing. Videoconferencing allows you to have face-to-face conversations with people on the Internet or on another network.

Your computer must have a sound card, speakers and a microphone to transmit and receive sound during a videoconference.

RESOLUTION AND SPEED

The resolution and speed of a Web camera determine the quality of images it can produce. Web cameras often offer several resolutions and speeds you can

choose from. Higher resolutions produce clearer and more detailed videos, though the videos transfer more slowly. A slow speed can cause a video to appear choppy.

Web cameras can commonly transfer videos at a speed of 15 frames per second and a resolution of 640 x 480 pixels or 30 frames per second at a resolution of 352 x 288 pixels.

SOFTWARE

Web cameras usually come with software that helps you set up and use the Web camera. You can often use this software to adjust the camera's settings, such as the brightness and contrast settings. A Web camera may also come with software that offers advanced features, such as video editing software.

ADDITIONAL FEATURES

Motion Sensing Capabilities

Some Web cameras have motion sensing capabilities, allowing the cameras to begin transferring or recording video when they detect movement. This is useful if you want to use a Web camera as a security camera.

Wireless Web Cameras

Some Web cameras do not need to be connected to a computer when transferring or recording videos. A wireless Web camera uses a transmitter to transfer a video to a receiver connected to the computer. These Web cameras must usually be within a certain range of the receiver to operate, such as 100 feet.

Digital Camera Capabilities

Most Web cameras have digital camera capabilities. This allows you to use the Web camera to take digital photos that you can use on your computer.

DIGITAL VIDEO CAMERA

A digital video camera records video in a format you can save on a computer.

DIGITAL VIDEO CAMERA ADVANTAGES

Quality

Digital videos are more clear and crisp than the analog videos a traditional video camera records. Unlike analog videos, digital videos do not suffer a loss in quality when copied.

Work With Videos

You can work with digital videos stored on your computer. For example, you can e-mail digital videos to friends, family and colleagues. You can also add digital videos to Web pages you create.

Edit Videos

You can use video editing software to edit videos saved on your computer. Some operating systems come with video editing software. For example, Windows Me includes the Windows Movie Maker program. You can also find video editing software at computer stores.

DIGITAL VIDEO CAMERA CONSIDERATIONS

Resolution

Digital video cameras use a device called a Charged Coupling Device (CCD) to capture video. The quality of video a digital video camera can produce depends on the amount of detail the CCD can detect. This detail, or resolution, is measured in pixels. The higher the number of pixels, the clearer and more detailed the video. Most digital video cameras have CCDs with a resolution between 250,000 and 700,000 pixels.

Storage

Most digital video cameras store videos on Mini DV (Digital Video) cassettes, which can store approximately one hour of video. The small size of a Mini DV cassette allows manufacturers to create digital video cameras that are smaller than other types of video cameras.

Features

Most digital video cameras have a color Liquid Crystal Display (LCD) screen, which is the same type of display found in notebook computers. The LCD screen lets you view what you are taping and preview videos you have recorded.

You may want to look for a digital video camera with additional features, such as a zoom lens or the ability to take digital photos.

GAME CONSOLE

A game console is a specialized computer system designed for playing video games.

Game consoles, also known as video game systems, connect to a television set.

Popular game console manufacturers include Sega, Sony, Nintendo and Microsoft.

POPULAR GAME CONSOLES

Sega Dreamcast, Sony PlayStation 2 and Nintendo 64 are currently popular game consoles. New game consoles include Nintendo Gamecube and Microsoft Xbox.

GAME CONSOLE GENERATIONS

Most game console manufacturers have released several generations of game consoles. Each new generation is more powerful and offers more features than the one before. For example, Sega's Dreamcast game console improves upon the previous Sega Saturn.

GAME CONSOLE ADVANTAGES

Game consoles are less expensive and easier to set up than a personal computer.

When purchasing games for a game console, you do not need to be concerned about hardware and software compatibility since the games for a console are specifically designed to work with the console.

GAME CONSOLE CONSIDERATIONS

Games

The games you can play on a game console depend on the console you use. You cannot play games designed for a different game console.

Games are commonly stored on Compact Discs (CDs) or cartridges. Some new game consoles can play games stored on Digital Versatile Discs (DVDs).

Game Controllers

Most game consoles come with one game controller. You can purchase additional game controllers to allow multiple people to play a game at once. The game controllers must be compatible with your game console.

Memory

Most game consoles require you to use a special memory card to store your progress in a game. Game consoles that use cartridges, such as Nintendo 64, may be able to store your progress on the cartridge. Microsoft Xbox has a built-in hard drive to store your progress.

Additional Features

Some game consoles, such as Sony PlayStation 2 and Microsoft Xbox, can also play music CDs and movies stored on DVDs.

The Sega Dreamcast game console has a built-in modem that allows you to play games with other people over the Internet.

INTERNET APPLIANCE

An Internet appliance is a device that allows you to access the Internet and exchange e-mail.

Using an Internet appliance is an economical way to access the Internet without having to buy a full-size computer.

Popular Internet appliances include Microsoft's MSN Companion, Compaq's iPAQ, Netpliance's i-opener and Oracle's New Internet Computer (NIC).

EASY TO SET UP AND USE

Internet appliances are easy for beginners to set up and use. In most cases, you only need to plug in the appliance and connect the modem to a phone line.

HARDWARE

Most Internet appliances include only the hardware necessary for accessing the Internet. For example, many Internet appliances consist of a screen, modem, keyboard, pointing device, CPU and memory.

An Internet appliance may also have ports, such as a printer port or USB port, that you can use to add devices to the appliance.

SOFTWARE

Internet appliances come with a Web browser and e-mail software you can use to access the Internet and exchange e-mail. Most Internet appliances use a version of the Microsoft Internet Explorer Web browser, though some Internet appliances use Netscape Navigator or a customized Web browser.

INTERNET SERVICE PROVIDER (ISP)

An ISP is a company that gives you access to the Internet. You must sign up with an ISP before you can use an Internet appliance. In most cases, you must pay a monthly fee for the ISP's services.

Many Internet appliances will only work with a particular ISP. For example, the iPAC Internet appliance requires you to use MSN Companion Service as your ISP. Some Internet appliances, such as the New Internet Computer, allow you to choose the ISP you want to use.

E-MAIL APPLIANCE

An e-mail appliance is similar to an Internet appliance, but is used only for sending and receiving e-mail messages. Landel Telecom's Mailbug is a popular e-mail appliance.

CONVERGENCE

As computer technology advances, it has begun to combine with other technologies. This combination of technologies is known as convergence.

EXAMPLES OF CONVERGENCE

Internet TV

Internet TV allows you to use your television to perform tasks on the Internet, such as sending e-mail and browsing the Web. Internet TV also allows you to take advantage of interactive TV, which lets you play along with game shows and vote in TV polls.

You need to sign-up with an Internet TV service, such as WebTV, to use Internet TV.

HDTV

High Definition Television (HDTV) produces images that are clearer than a regular television set. Instead of using analog signals, HDTV uses digital signals similar to those used by a computer. This allows the television screen to display a much higher resolution. Only a few television stations currently broadcast digital signals for HDTV.

Digital Video Recorders

A Digital Video Recorder (DVR) digitally records television shows on a hard drive. This allows you to control the way you watch television. For example, you can play an instant replay during a show or pause a show and then continue watching the show later.

To use a DVR, you need to sign-up with service that offers DVR. TiVo and ReplayTV are popular DVR services.

Appliance Controls

Appliance controls let you control the appliances in your home using a computer system. For example, you can buy software that lets you control electrical appliances such as coffee pots, ceiling fans and lamps from your computer.

Internet Radio

You use an Internet radio to connect to the Internet and listen to radio stations that broadcast over the Internet. This allows you to listen to stations you would not normally be able to receive, such as stations in Australia. Kerbango manufactured the first Internet radio.

Wireless Devices

What is a PDA? How can I access the Internet using a mobile phone? Learn about wireless devices in this chapter.

INTRODUCTION TO WIRELESS DEVICES

Wireless devices can access information on the Internet or another network without using a phone line or other physical connection.

TYPES OF WIRELESS DEVICES

Notebook Computers

Notebook computers can use a wireless modem to access information on the Internet or on another network. If your notebook computer does not have a wireless modem, you may be able to use a mobile phone with a standard modem to wirelessly connect to a network.

Personal Digital Assistants

Many Personal Digital Assistants (PDAs) now offer wireless Internet capabilities, allowing you to access information on the Internet and exchange e-mail. Some PDAs can connect to a wireless network using a radio transceiver. Many PDAs can wirelessly exchange information with other PDAs using infrared signals.

Mobile Phones

Many companies now incorporate Internet features into their mobile phones. For example, you can use most new mobile phones to access e-mail messages and find text-based information on the Internet. Internet access for a mobile phone is provided by the same company that provides the telephone service.

Two-way Pagers

Two-way pagers are small, handheld devices that allow you to exchange e-mail messages with other people. These devices specialize in text messaging, though they can sometimes perform more complex functions such as browsing the Web. RIM's BlackBerry is a popular two-way pager.

Automobile Devices

Some companies are developing wireless devices that work with, or replace, the radio and audio systems found in automobiles. These new devices will allow the occupants of an automobile to use voice commands to access information on the Internet, such as up-to-the-minute traffic reports and driving directions.

INTRODUCTION TO WIRELESS DEVICES

Up-to-date Information

Most wireless devices allow you to access information on the Internet. This lets you find up-to-date information such as weather reports, stock quotes and price lists while you are away from your computer. Wireless devices are also commonly used to access information on a company network while traveling.

Navigation

Some wireless devices, such as PDAs and notebook computers, can display maps of cities and streets to help users navigate around an unfamiliar area. Wireless devices can also access traffic reports from the Internet and suggest alternative routes to avoid traffic congestion.

mCommerce

mCommerce, or mobile commerce, is a system that allows you to use a wireless device to purchase products and services on the Internet. mCommerce is useful for purchasing airline tickets and hotel accommodations, although you can purchase almost any product or service online.

E-mail and Instant Messaging

Most wireless devices allow users to send e-mail messages to communicate with friends and colleagues.

Some wireless devices offer instant messaging capabilities. This allows you to see when your friends and colleagues are online and send them instant text messages.

Access Software

Many large companies have developed their own software, such as an invoicing or order placing program. Adapting these programs to work with wireless devices provides employees with immediate access to the software, even if they are away from the office. For example, a salesperson can use a wireless device to access an invoicing program while traveling.

Multimedia

Some wireless devices, such as mobile phones and PDAs, now include multimedia software that allows you to access, store and play multimedia files, such as MP3 music files. There are many music Web sites, such as www.mp3.com, which allow you to download music files to a wireless device.

WIRELESS NETWORKING

The devices on a wireless network, such as notebook computers and mobile phones, can access information on the network without being physically connected to the network.

RADIO SIGNALS

Wireless networks use radio signals to transmit information between the devices on the network. A wireless network can transfer information at a speed of up to 11 Mbps.

RADIO TRANSCEIVERS

All wireless devices include a radio transceiver, which enables the devices to exchange information on a network. Some wireless devices have transceivers connected to the outside of the device, while other wireless devices have built-in transceivers.

WIRELESS NETWORK ADVANTAGES

A wireless network eliminates the cables that connect the devices on a traditional network. This helps reduce clutter and is useful for connecting computers in different areas of a building. Wireless networks also allow mobile devices, such as notebook computers, to remain connected to the network when they are moved from one area to another.

WIRELESS LOCAL AREA NETWORK

A wireless Local Area Network (LAN) is a wireless network that connects computers and devices within a small geographic area, such as a building.

Wireless LANs are useful for businesses, since they allow a company to set up a network that employees can access from almost anywhere in a building.

Wireless home networking kits are also available that allow you to create a wireless LAN in your home. Wireless home networks are commonly used to share a high-speed Internet connection between several computers or play multi-player games.

WIRELESS PERSONAL AREA NETWORK

A Wireless Personal Area Network (WPAN) is a short-range network that allows wireless devices to exchange information with each other. For example, when you transfer a contact's phone number from a mobile phone to a PDA, you are using a WPAN.

To successfully exchange information using a WPAN, the wireless devices must use the same transmission technology. A WPAN standard is currently in development that will ensure different wireless devices will be able to communicate with each other.

WIRELESS OPERATING SYSTEMS

An operating system is the software that controls the overall activity of a device. All wireless devices require an operating system to function.

EMBEDDED

Most wireless devices use an embedded operating system. An embedded operating system is stored on a chip inside the device, instead of on a hard drive or other erasable storage device. Embedded operating systems cannot usually be upgraded to newer versions without replacing the entire device.

SOFTWARE

An operating system runs all the software for a device, such as scheduling and messaging programs. Software designed for one wireless operating system will not work with another wireless operating system. Depending on the wireless operating system you use, you may be able to install additional software to add features to the device.

POPULAR WIRELESS OPERATING SYSTEMS

Palm OS

Palm OS is the most popular operating system for Personal Digital Assistants (PDAs). The Palm OS operating system was developed by Palm Inc. with a special focus on features that were important to PDA users. Some PDAs manufactured by other companies, such as Handspring, also use Palm OS.

Windows CE

Windows CE is a version of the Microsoft Windows operating system developed specifically for PDAs. The main advantage of using Windows CE is that information can be easily exchanged with other Microsoft programs, such as Microsoft Word. PDAs that use Windows CE are often referred to as Pocket PCs.

EPOC

The EPOC operating system was developed by manufacturers of mobile phones. This operating system is commonly used on mobile phones that offer Internet capabilities, though it is also sometimes used on other devices, such as some PDAs.

PERSONAL DIGITAL ASSISTANT

Most new Personal Digital Assistants (PDAs) offer wireless Internet capabilities.

Palm Inc. and Handspring are companies that manufacture PDAs you can use to wirelessly access the Internet.

INTERNET CAPABILITIES

Some PDAs come with built-in Internet capabilities. If your PDA does not already have Internet capabilities, you may be able to add a wireless modem to the PDA. You can check with the manufacturer of your PDA to determine if a wireless modem is available for the PDA.

SERVICE PROVIDER

The service provider you will use to access the Internet depends on the type of PDA you use. When choosing a PDA, you should determine the coverage area of the service provider to make sure that you will be able to access the Internet at home, at work and while traveling, depending on your needs. You should also make sure you understand how the service provider will bill you for the time you spend online.

WEB PAGES

Many PDAs can only display Web pages that are designed for wireless devices. Companies such as Yahoo!, Amazon.com and CNN.com have designed versions of their Web pages for wireless devices.

Some new PDAs with larger screens allow you to view the same Web pages you can view using a full-size computer.

INPUT INFORMATION

Most PDAs come with an electronic pen, called a stylus, that you can use to input information. Some PDAs can even recognize handwriting, allowing you to write the information you want to input directly on the screen.

ADDITIONAL FEATURES

PDAs offer more features than many other wireless devices. For example, you can use a PDA to manage contacts, schedule appointments and create memos, as well as exchange e-mail messages, shop online and browse the Web.

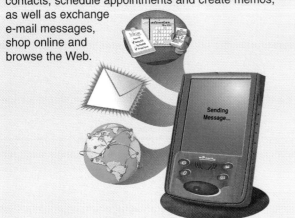

SCREEN

A PDA has a larger screen than most other wireless devices. This allows you to view more information on the screen at once. Some PDAs come with color screens, enhancing the appearance of information you view on the Internet.

MOBILE PHONE

Mobile phones are quickly becoming one of the easiest and most popular ways to wirelessly access the Internet.

You can use a mobile phone to exchange e-mail messages, browse the Web, shop online, make phone calls and more.

INTERNET ACCESS

To access the Internet using a mobile phone, the phone must be Internet-enabled and your service provider must offer Internet access.

Keep in mind that some service providers can send information such as stock quotes and sports scores to your mobile phone without connecting the phone to the Internet. You should make sure that your service provider will connect your phone to the Internet.

MINIBROWSER

Most Internet-enabled mobile phones use a specialized Web browser, called a minibrowser. You can use a minibrowser to view information on Web pages, select links and bookmark your favorite Web pages. Minibrowsers cannot perform advanced functions, such as displaying complex graphics.

COST

Internet access for a mobile phone is usually an additional service that you must pay extra for. There are several ways your service provider can bill you for the time you spend online. For example, some service providers bill by the minute, as though you were making a regular phone call. To avoid unexpected charges, make sure you understand the billing method your service provider uses.

COVERAGE AREA

You should check your service provider's coverage area to make sure you will be able to access the Internet from your home area and from any areas you frequently travel to.

WEB PAGES

When browsing the Web using a mobile phone, you can only access Web pages that are designed for wireless devices. Companies such as Yahoo!, Amazon.com and CNN.com have designed versions of their Web sites for wireless devices.

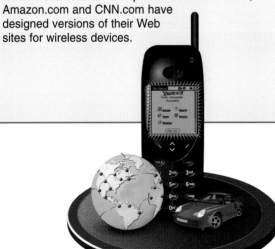

SCREEN SIZE

Most mobile phones currently have small screens, allowing you to view only a few lines of text at a time. Future models of Internet-enabled mobile phones will offer larger screen sizes.

TWO-WAY PAGER

A two-way pager is a small, handheld device that allows you to send and receive short e-mail messages.

Popular two-way pagers include Motorola's Talkabout T900 and RIM's BlackBerry.

SERVICE PLAN

After you buy a two-way pager, you must sign up for a monthly service plan before you can use the pager. Companies that sell two-way pagers usually offer a selection of service plans you can choose from.

Some service plans allow you to exchange an unlimited number of messages each month for a set fee. Other plans specify the maximum number of messages you can exchange in a month, charging you extra for any additional messages.

COVERAGE AREA

Before choosing a two-way pager, you should check the company's service area to make sure that you will be able to use the pager at home, at work and while traveling, depending on your needs. Some companies allow you to choose between a local or national service plan.

KEYBOARD SIZE

Two-way pagers have a small, built-in keyboard that you can use to type messages. The keyboard's small size can make composing messages time-consuming. For this reason, two-way pagers are most often used for exchanging short messages.

SCREEN SIZE

Many two-way pagers have small screens, allowing you to view only a few lines of text at a time. If you frequently send longer messages, you may want to use a two-way pager that has a larger screen.

SPEED

Two-way pagers are generally slower than other wireless devices. For example, a message you send using a two-way pager usually takes longer to be delivered than a message you send using a mobile phone.

ADVANCED FEATURES

Some two-way pagers offer advanced features such as scheduling programs and fax capabilities.

A two-way pager may also allow you to access information on the Internet, such as news, sports and weather.

Visual Glossary

GIF Image

GIF (Graphics Interchange Format) images are often used for logos, banners and computer-generated art on Web pages. A GIF image can contain up to 256 colors. GIF image files have the .gif extension (example: banner.gif).

JPEG Image

JPEG (Joint Photographic Experts Group) images are usually used for photographs and very large images. A JPEG image can contain approximately 16.7 million colors while maintaining a small file size. This allows a JPEG image to transfer quickly over the Internet. JPEG image files usually have the .jpg extension (example: photo.jpg).

Hacker

A hacker is a person who enjoys programming computers. This term is often used incorrectly by the media to describe a cracker.

Information Technology

Information Technology (IT) is a term used to describe the technologies associated with managing information. Software, networking and Internet-related technologies are examples of Information Technology. This term is also often used to describe careers in the computing industry.

JSP

JSP (JavaServer Pages) is a technology developed by Sun Microsystems that allows you to create dynamic Web pages by using the Java programming language within the Web pages.

IP Address

Every computer connected to the Internet has a unique number, called an Internet Protocol (IP) address. The IP address is made up of four different numbers separated by periods, such as 554.234.123.85.

KDE

K Desktop Environment (KDE) is a Graphical User Interface (GUI) used on UNIX and Linux operating systems. KDE allows you to use pictures to perform tasks instead of typing text at the command line.

Mirror

Some ... stores exactly ... but is usually ... geographically ... provide a faster and ...

.NET

.NET is a collection of technologies created by Microsoft to bring together networking components commonly used by businesses.

CHAPTER 16

Visual Glossary

Do you want to know what the terms "bandwidth" and "cookie" mean? Find the definitions for interesting and useful computer terms in this glossary.

404 Not Found

The 404 Not Found error message appears when your Web browser cannot find a Web page you tried to display. The Web page may have moved or the name of the Web page may have changed.

802.11

802.11, also called Wireless Ethernet, is a standard that specifies how information should transfer on a wireless network. Most wireless devices use the 802.11 standard.

AirPort

AirPort is a technology developed by Apple Computer that allows you to set up a wireless network using Macintosh computers.

Application Service Provider

An Application Service Provider (ASP) is a company that stores software on a server people can access over the Internet. This allows people to use the software without having to store the software on their computer.

ASCII

ASCII (American Standard Code for Information Interchange) is a numbering system that assigns numerical values to letters, numbers and other characters. Many programs save, read and exchange data using the ASCII numbering system.

ASP

ASP (Active Server Pages) is a technology developed by Microsoft that is used to create powerful and dynamic Web pages and sophisticated Web applications.

Bandwidth

Bandwidth describes the rate at which information on a network can transfer. The wider the bandwidth of a network, the more information can be transferred at once.

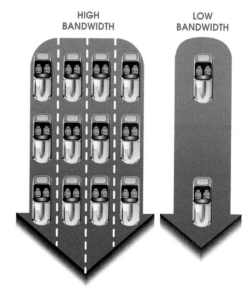

HIGH BANDWIDTH   LOW BANDWIDTH

Bcc

A Bcc (Blind carbon copy) is an exact copy of an e-mail message. You can send a Bcc to a person without the other recipients knowing that the person received the message.

Beta Software

Beta software is an early version of a software product that is not quite ready for sale. Beta software is often distributed so that people will test the software and report any problems or suggest improvements to the manufacturer.

Bluetooth

Bluetooth is a new standard for wireless technology that will be used to exchange information over short distances. The Bluetooth standard specifies how different wireless devices will exchange data with each other, with desktop computers and with networks.

Broadband

Broadband is the high-speed transmission of multiple types of information, such as video and audio.

Bug

A bug is an error in a hardware device or software program. Some bugs are harmless, such as bugs that display the wrong image or a spelling error on the screen. Other bugs are more serious, such as bugs that prevent a device or program from operating.

C and C++

C and C++ are high-level programming languages. These languages are commonly used to develop operating systems and application software.

Cc

A Cc (Carbon Copy) is an exact copy of an e-mail message. You can send a carbon copy to a person who is not directly involved, but would be interested in the message.

CDMA

CDMA (Code Division Multiple Access) is a technology used to transfer information between wireless devices.

CGI Script

A CGI (Common Gateway Interface) script is a program that a Web server runs to process information. CGI scripts are commonly used to process the information people enter when they fill out a form on a Web page.

Concryption

Concryption is the process of encrypting and compressing data. Concryption is useful when sending information over a network. Encryption scrambles the data to prevent unauthorized access and compression allows the data to transfer faster over a network.

Cookie

Some Web sites use cookies to keep track of people who access the site. For example, when you visit a Web site, the site may create a cookie to store your name. The next time you visit the Web site, the site may display your name on the page.

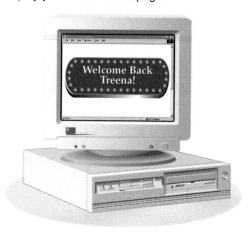

Cracker

A cracker is a person who breaks into computers and networks with the intention of causing damage, such as deleting files.

Default Settings

The settings that are originally turned on in a computer program are referred to as the default settings. For example, a word processor has a default font setting it automatically uses each time you create a new document.

DHTML

DHTML (Dynamic HTML) is a combination of Web page creation technologies, including JavaScript and HTML. DHTML allows you to create complex animated and interactive Web pages that do not need to be processed by a Web server.

E-commerce

E-commerce is a term that refers to conducting business online. For example, when you buy or sell a product or service online, you are participating in e-commerce. E-commerce is sometimes referred to as e-business.

Encryption

Encryption is the process of scrambling information to prevent unauthorized people from accessing the information. This is useful when transferring information over the Internet or another network.

Flash

Flash is a program that allows you to create animation effects and interactive features for Web pages.

Footprint

The footprint of a device is the amount of space the device takes up on your desk. The smaller the footprint, the less desk space the device occupies.

Force Feedback

Force feedback is a feature offered by some game controllers, such as joysticks and gamepads. A force feedback game controller moves in response to actions in a game, creating a more realistic playing experience.

FTP Program

An FTP (File Transfer Protocol) program allows you to transfer information to a Web server so that it will be available on the Web. For example, you can use an FTP program to transfer Web pages you create to a Web server. Popular FTP programs include WS_FTP Pro for Windows and Fetch for Macintosh.

FTP Site

An FTP (File Transfer Protocol) site is a site on the Internet that stores a collection of files that people can download, or copy, to their computers.

GIF Image

GIF (Graphics Interchange Format) images are often used for logos, banners and computer-generated art on Web pages. A GIF image can contain up to 256 colors. GIF image files have the .gif extension (example: banner.gif).

Hacker

A hacker is a person who enjoys programming computers. This term is often used incorrectly by the media to describe a cracker.

Information Technology

Information Technology (IT) is a term used to describe the technologies associated with managing information. Software, networking and Internet-related technologies are examples of Information Technology. This term is also often used to describe careers in the computing industry.

IP Address

Every computer connected to the Internet has a unique number, called an Internet Protocol (IP) address. The IP address is made up of four different numbers separated by periods, such as 254.234.123.65.

JPEG Image

JPEG (Joint Photographic Experts Group) images are usually used for photographs and very large images. A JPEG image can contain approximately 16.7 million colors while maintaining a small file size. This allows a JPEG image to transfer quickly over the Internet. JPEG image files usually have the .jpg extension (example: photo.jpg).

JSP

JSP (Java Server Pages) is a technology developed by Sun Microsystems that allows you to create dynamic Web pages by using the Java programming language within the Web pages.

KDE

K Desktop Environment (KDE) is a Graphical User Interface (GUI) used on UNIX and Linux operating systems. KDE allows you to use pictures to perform tasks instead of typing text at the command line.

MIME

The Multi-purpose Internet Mail Extension (MIME) allows you to attach programs, pictures and sounds to your e-mail messages and newsgroup articles. Most e-mail and newsgroup programs allow you to send and receive MIME attachments.

Mirror Sites

Some popular Web sites have mirror sites. A mirror site stores exactly the same information as the original site, but is usually less busy. A mirror site may also be geographically closer to your computer, which can provide a faster and more reliable connection.

.NET

.NET is a collection of technologies created by Microsoft to bring together networking components commonly used by businesses.

Newbie

A newbie is a person who is new to the Internet. The Internet is so vast that newbies often get lost and need help from more experienced users. Newbie is sometimes considered a derogatory term.

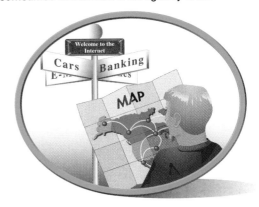

Overclocking

Overclocking refers to increasing the speed of a CPU above the speed the manufacturer intended for the CPU. Overclocking is not recommended, since it can result in unreliable performance.

PC System Design Guide

The PC System Design Guide is a guideline created by Intel and Microsoft that outlines the hardware that should be included on new computers.

Perl

Perl (Practical Extraction and Report Language) is a popular, high-level Web programming language. Perl is useful for processing information entered into a form on a Web page.

PHP

PHP is a scripting language used to create powerful and dynamic Web pages. PHP can run on a variety of operating systems and can easily work with many different applications, such as Web servers and database programs.

Proxy Server

Some networks use a proxy server that individual computers on the network must go through to access the Internet. Proxy servers are useful for filtering out information. For example, a company network can use a proxy server to control the Web sites employees can access.

Ricochet

Ricochet is a high-speed wireless network. A Ricochet network is created by placing wireless radio devices in various locations throughout an area, such as on streetlights and utility poles in a city. Wireless devices that use Ricochet modems can use the radio devices to connect to the network. Ricochet networks are currently used in many large urban areas in North America.

Shockwave

Shockwave is a type of plug-in, or helper program, that you can install to allow your Web browser to display the interactive animations used on some Web pages.

Source Code

The source code of a Web page is the code used to create the Web page. Viewing the source code for a Web page is an excellent way to learn how the Web page was created.

Virtual Reality

Virtual reality is a 3D computer-generated reality. To experience virtual reality, you wear special goggles that make you feel as though you are in the virtual world. Virtual reality is used for some games and for career training, such as flight simulation training.

Virus Hoax

A virus hoax is an untrue rumor about a computer virus. Many e-mail virus warnings on the Internet are virus hoaxes.

W3C

The W3C (World Wide Web Consortium) is made up of hundreds of organizations that have an interest in the future of the World Wide Web. The W3C sets the standards for various Web-related technologies, such as HTML.

WAP

WAP (Wireless Application Protocol) is a set of languages that allow wireless devices to access the Internet. WAP was developed by several large manufacturers of wireless devices to ensure that products created by different companies would be able to work together. Wireless devices that use WAP to access the Internet are commonly referred to as WAP-enabled devices.

Web Hosting Service

Web hosting services are companies that store Web pages you create and make them available on the Web.

Webcast

A webcast is live audio or video sent over the Internet. Examples of webcasts include sound from a live press conference and video from a traffic camera.

Webmaster

A Webmaster is the person in charge of maintaining a Web site. A Webmaster is sometimes called a Web Administrator, Site Administrator or Content Editor.

WML

WML (Wireless Markup Language) is a computer language used to create Web pages that can be displayed on wireless devices. Only wireless devices that are WAP-enabled can display Web pages created using WML.

XML

XML (eXtensible Markup Language) is a computer language that allows Web page authors to create their own markup languages. XML has more rigid rules for creating Web pages than HTML.

INDEX

INDEX

GUI (Graphical User Interface)
  in handheld computer, 165
  in KDE, 288
  in Linux, 149
  in Mac OS X, 151
  in Macintosh computer, 169
  in Windows, 135

H

hacker, 288
handheld
  computer, 164-165
  pointing device, 24
  scanner, 59
handshake, in modem, 55
hard drive, 10, 82-89
  in notebook computer, 160
hardware, 4
  game, 131
  Internet appliance, 262
HDTV (High Definition Television), convergence, 264
headphones, 95
help
  documentation, 5
  software, 109
Help Web pages, Linux, 148
high-speed Internet connection, 56-57
history list, as Web browser feature, 209
home
  network, 180
  page, 209
Home directory, in Linux, 148
Home Networking Wizard, as Windows Me feature, 142
hot plug, 65
  FireWire, 67
hot swapping, 65
  FireWire, 67
HTML (HyperText Markup Language), 222
http (HyperText Transfer Protocol), 207
https, 219
hub, 183
hyperlink, Web page, 207, 223
Hz (hertz)
  refresh rate, 40
  speaker frequency, 62

I

i.LINK, 66
iBook, 174
IEEE 1394, 66
iMac, 172-173
image
  add
    to document, using word processor, 113
    to Web page, 223
  scan, 58
image editing software, 58, 254
image editor, 122-123
image file, format. See specific file type.
imaging device, in Macintosh computer, 177

information
  analyze, in database, 118
  archive, 89
  exchange
    in handheld computer, 165
    on network, 186-187
  find
    in database, 120
    using Web portal, 212
  inappropriate, Web, and children, 220
  on Internet, access, 194
  management program, in application suite, 127
  query, in database, 120
  sort, in database, 120
  store, in database, 118
  transfers, on the Internet, 196-197
Information Superhighway, 192
Information Technology (IT), 288
infrared port, 163
ink-jet printer, 34-35
input
  device, 6
    in handheld computer, 164
    in Macintosh computer, 176-177
    in notebook computer, 158-159
  information in PDA, 277
insert CD-ROM disc, 95
insertion point, in word processor, 111
inside
  computer, 10-11
  floppy drive, 90
install
  programs, using CD-ROM drive, 93
  software, 108
instant messaging
  program, 248-249
  wireless device application, 271
intercast technology, as tv tuner card feature, 51
internal
  cache, 76
  modem, 53
  removable storage device, 102
Internet, 192-193
  in Mac OS 9, 150
  in Windows 98, 141
Internet access
  using handheld computer, 165
  using Macintosh computer, 173
  using mobile phone, 278
Internet appliance, 262-263
Internet capabilities, PDA, 276
Internet Connection Wizard, 198
Internet Explorer, Windows 98, 140
Internet radio, convergence, 265
Internet TV, convergence, 264
intranet, 189
IP address, 288
IRC (Internet Relay Chat), 247
ISA (Industry Standard Architecture) bus, 79
ISDN (Integrated Services Digital Network) line, 57
ISP (Internet Service Provider), 198, 200-203
  using Internet appliance, 263
IT (Information Technology), 288

INDEX

S

sampling rate, in sound card, 48
save files, on hard drive, 83
scan
    image, 58
    mode, 60
    text, 58
ScanDisk program, in MS-DOS, 137
Scanner, 58-61. *See also specific scanner type.*
screen, 38
    burn, 42
    in notebook computer, 154, 156-157
    PDA, 277
    saver, 42
    size
        in mobile phone, 279
        in notebook computer, 156
        in two-way pager, 281
scroll, in word processor, 111
SCSI (Small Computer System Interface), 85
SDRAM (Synchronous DRAM), 71
search tool, 210-211
    using Web browser, 210
sectors, 90
secure Web site, 219
security
    network, 188
    in UNIX, 147
send
    e-mail message, 230
    fax, 53
    newsgroup message, privately, 244
serial port, 15
server
    on client/server network, 185
    Web, 206
service plan, two-way pager, 280
service provider, PDA, 276
set up Internet appliance, 262
set-top box, 8
sheet-fed scanner, 59
shielded speakers, 63
Shockwave, 290
shopping
    Web, 218-219
    Web portal, 212
shortcut, in Windows 95, 139
shouting, in e-mail message, 231
signature, as e-mail feature, 230
SIMM (Single In-Line Memory Module), 71
site
    FTP, 287
    Web, 206
size
    image, in desktop publishing, 125
    memory, 70
    monitor, 39
    screen, in notebook computer, 156

slot, expansion, 10, 16
smiley, in e-mail message, 231
snail mail, 227
software, 4. *See also* application; program.
    application, 4
    beta, 285
    bundled, 109
    CD-R and CR-RW, 97
    game, 130-131
    get, 108
    groupware, 182
    help, 109
    iMac, 173
    image editing, 58, 254
    install, 108
    Internet appliance, 263
    intranet, 189
    ISP, 203
    in Linux, 149
    OCR, 58
    operating system, 4
    overview, 4, 108-109
    patch, 109
    removable storage device, 102
    run, as operating system function, 134
    update, 109
    utility, 128-129
    version, 109
    video editing, 258
    Web camera, 257
    wireless operating system, 274
solid-state device, 252
sort information, in database, 120
sound
    capabilities, Macintosh computer, 177
    card, 17, 46-49
        in notebook computer, 159
    record, 46
source code, 290
speaker, 9, 46, 62-63
    jack, sound card, 47
    in notebook computer, 159
    port, Macintosh computer, 175
special characters, keyboard, 31
speed
    ATM, 187
    bus, 78
    CD-R and CD-RW, 96
    CD-ROM, 94
    CPU, 73
    DVD-ROM, 99
    e-mail, 227
    Ethernet, 186
    FireWire, 67
    hard drive, 84
    ink-jet printer, 34
    laser printer, 36
    modem, 54

Read Less, Learn More™

Visual

Simplified®

Simply the Easiest Way to Learn

For visual learners who are brand-new to a topic and want to be shown, not told, how to solve a problem in a friendly, approachable way.

All *Simplified*® books feature friendly Disk characters who demonstrate and explain the purpose of each task.

Title	ISBN	Price
America Online® Simplified®, 2nd Ed.	0-7645-3433-5	$24.99
Computers Simplified®, 4th Ed.	0-7645-6042-5	$24.99
Creating Web Pages with HTML Simplified®, 2nd Ed.	0-7645-6067-0	$24.99
Excel 97 Simplified®	0-7645-6022-0	$24.99
Excel for Windows® 95 Simpified®	1-56884-682-7	$19.99
FrontPage® 2000® Simplified®	0-7645-3450-5	$24.99
Internet and World Wide Web Simplified®, 3rd Ed.	0-7645-3409-2	$24.99
Lotus® 1-2-3® Release 5 for Windows® Simplified®	1-56884-670-3	$19.99
Microsoft® Access 2000 Simplified®	0-7645-6058-1	$24.99
Microsoft® Excel 2000 Simplified®	0-7645-6053-0	$24.99
Microsoft® Office 2000 Simplified®	0-7645-6052-2	$29.99
Microsoft® Word 2000 Simplified®	0-7645-6054-9	$24.99
More Windows® 95 Simplified®	1-56884-689-4	$19.99
More Windows® 98 Simplified®	0-7645-6037-9	$24.99
Office 97 Simplified®	0-7645-6009-3	$29.99
PC Upgrade and Repair Simplified®	0-7645-6049-2	$24.99
Windows® 95 Simplified®	1-56884-662-2	$19.99
Windows® 98 Simplified®	0-7645-6030-1	$24.99
Windows® 2000 Professional Simplified®	0-7645-3422-X	$24.99
Windows® Me Millennium Edition Simplified®	0-7645-3494-7	$24.99
Word 97 Simplified®	0-7645-6011-5	$24.99